Quest for Sanctity

Seven Passages to Growth in Faith

Quest for Sanctity

Seven Passages to Growth in Faith

by

Gerald R. Grosh, S.J.

Michael Glazier, Inc.
1935 W. Fourth St., Wilmington, DE 19805

About the Author

Rev. Gerald R. Grosh, S.J., received his Ph.D. in theology from Fordham University in 1972. He helped found the Jesuit Renewal Center in Milford, Ohio and has served as the Rector of the Jesuit Community of Loyola University of Chicago. Father Grosh is currently involved in pastoral ministry with the Hispanic Community in Moline, Illinois.

First published in 1988 by Michael Glazier, Inc., 1935 West Fourth Street, Wilmington, Delaware 19805.

Library of Congress Catalog Card Number: 87-82352
International Standard Book Number: 0-89453-635-4

Printed by Edwards Brothers, Ann Arbor, Michigan.
Typography by Angela Meades.
Printed in the United States of America.

TABLE OF CONTENTS

Part II: Faith in a Personal God

1

ORIENTATION

Faith is a gift—a gift from the Lord. Each person follows his own unique path of growth in faith because the Lord loves each person uniquely. The process in which each person grows in relationship with God is such a mystery that it seems almost a travesty to try to chart the course. Yet the human mind wants to know; we have an innate drive to understand.

This book treats seven passages through which most people pass as they grow in faith. This book captures the experience of doing spiritual direction and training spiritual directors at the Jesuit Renewal Center in Milford Ohio—an exciting experience in which the staff learned much about human nature, the life of faith, and the nature of our relationship with God. Though the book aims to help spiritual directors and those who train spiritual directors, I hope that the language and style are simple and concrete enough to stimulate any person who desires spiritual growth.

A revolution has dawned in the religious consciousness of Americans in the last twenty years occasioned both by religion and by the development of psychology. A renewed interest in spirituality and in spiritual growth has emerged, as exemplified in the rediscovery of Eastern religions and the interest in transcendental meditation and prayer. But, perhaps, the most significant expression of the resurgence of spirituality has been the renewed interest in the *Spiritual Exercises* of St. Ignatius and in the emergence of the personally directed retreat. The author of this book has been a part of this movement almost from the beginning of its rebirth. This book is the product of his experience.

Three notions undergird the experience and reflections of this book: experience, desire, and development. Many authors have spun theories about these notions which are most crucial to spirituality and to the expositions within this book.

The role of experience

The present religious renewal represents a radical reappraisal of many of the theological understandings that flourished before 1960, at least within Roman Catholic circles. In 1960 the Catholic Church had a clear set of rules and dogmas, which it considered absolute truths offering little possibility for further development, nuance, or articulation. It was apparent that these statements conflicted with statements from other religions and other branches of human knowledge, especially psychology. Varying viewpoints argued against each other on the rational level, with little meeting of minds. In the sixties disagreement began to give way to dialogue as divergent groups searched for a common experience that might have given rise to the different formulations.

The foundation for such an approach was already laid by

John Dewey[1] in American philosophy and William James[2] in his analysis of religious experience. Robert Johann[3] began to bridge Thomistic concepts and the American philosophical and theological perspective. He noted that not only did our understanding have to rise out of our experience but it had to return to experience for its validation. Bernard Lonergan[4] clearly articulated this position in his monumental work *Insight*. Such a process makes experience the human starting point and momentary finishing point in one's search for understanding.

Within Roman Catholicism there grew a new importance for the role of experience. Many Roman Catholics began to accept that a particular dogma attempted to conceptualize a given religious experience or series of religious experiences and that scripture portrayed the faith experience of the early Christians. Theologians articulated a theology of revelation which, instead of emphasizing that God's revelation ended with the death of the last apostle, opened the doors for God's continuing revelation in the *now* experiences of individuals, the Church, and the world. The Christian was called not only to listen to the signs of the times in the world, but also to his

---

[1] John Dewey, *Art as Experience* (New York, 1939); *Experience and Education* (New York, 1938); *Experience and Nature* (LaSalle, 1929).

[2] William James, *The Varieties of Religious Experience: A Study in Human Nature* (New York, 1902).

[3] Robert Johann, *Building the Human* (New York, 1968); *The Meaning of Love* (Glen Rock, 1966).

[4] Bernard J. Lonergan, *Insight: A Study of Human Understanding* (New York, 1970).

own inner experience to find out what God was saying in his or her life.

The author has participated in this latter movement. He has taken seriously God's ongoing revelation, i.e., that God speaks now in the reality of our experiences, in our thoughts, feelings, hopes, fears, and desires. He has called others to look to the reality of their experience as the locus for God's revelation. Most people do not want to accept their experiences, or, at least, certain experiences. They would rather deny or hide such feelings as anger, hurt, envy, resentment, doubt of faith, or sexual attractions. The author believes that no experience is foreign to the touch of God and, in fact, that it is in the very experiences which we would prefer not to have that God strives to draw us to Himself.

Importance of desire

When we listen to our experience, we discover various desires which motivate our actions. Rather than judge these as "selfish" and try to go against them, the author has discovered that desires capture the essence of a person and should be trusted, contrary to past teaching which called Christians to suppress their own wants in order to seek God's will.

God's will takes shape in the specific desires of a person. Our desires manifest our loves and values and give shape to our unique participation in God. They manifest the way we express ourselves and actualize our own unique images of God.

Desires surface at different levels. For example: I can desire to go for a run. I can desire a good steak for my evening meal. I can desire to be a good husband, a good mother, or a good religious. I can desire to succeed at my work. I can desire to love. I can desire union with God. I can desire to do God's will. Some of these desires are more superficial; other desires capture the core of the person.

The deepest desire of a person is "the governing grace." Frequently, it takes some time before a person recognizes his or her deepest desire. As his primary task, the spiritual director helps a person name his deepest desire and gives suggestions as to how he might fulfill his deepest desire.

The governing grace flows like a deep current in a river. There may be all sorts of currents, but the governing grace is the deepest current within us; it is the power of the spirit. It shifts from time to time in a person's life and changes its character. At one time, a person yearns for one thing, at another time for something else. The various chapters of this book center around some of the deepest desires that a person can experience and the passages through which one moves in fulfilling these desires.

A spiritual director helps a person get in touch with his or her deepest desire. Often enough, this is facilitated by the person's having to make a concrete decision. God often uses a concrete decision to surface within the person the new choice or challenge, the cutting edge of his or her growth. The actual decision or choice matters little; what counts is the underlying call to personal growth, to relationship with God, i.e., the governing grace, which surfaces as the person faces the challenge involved in this decision. The author believes that the governing grace is the power of the Holy Spirit leading this person to make a decision. It is the *governing* grace, because it "controls" this decision. In fact, it controls the spiritual life at any given moment. It is already flowing within the person; one's task is to get in touch with that flow. The governing grace is the deepest and most active truth about the person.

A *developmental approach*

The author has a third presupposition in this book: a person grows in the spiritual life in patterns that can be charted. Today numerous authors have popularized various developmental theories. Piaget[5] has focused on a child's learning development. Erikson[6] has written of personality development. Kohlberg[7] has articulated a developmental theory concerning a person's moral growth. Fowler,[8] taking off from Kohlberg, has delineated a theory about the cognitive structures of faith development. Levinson[9] and Sheehy[10] have written about stages of development in the process of male and female maturation. All these theories of developmental process

[5]Jean Piaget, *The Essential Piaget*, edited by Howard E. Guber and J. Jacques Voneche (New York, 1977).

[6]Erik Erikson, *Identity and the Life Cycle* (New York, 1959); *Adulthood: Essays* (New York, 1978); *Identity, Youth, and Crisis* (New York, 1968); *Childhood and Selfhood* (New York, 1978).

[7]Lawrence Kohlberg, *The Philosophy of Moral Development* (New York, 1981), especially pp. 409-412.

[8]James W. Fowler, *Stages of Faith: The Psychology of Human Development and the Quest for Meaning* (New York, 1981).

[9]Daniel J. Levinson, *The Season's of a Man's Life* (New York, 1978).

[10]Gail Sheehy, *Passages: Predictable Crises of Adult Life* (New York, 1976).

highlight the understanding of the human person as someone who is in constant process.

In his ministry with the spiritual lives of others, the author has recognized these psychological, moral, and faith developmental processes. In addition, he has noted a spiritual developmental process. He does not offer a new insight; Soren Kierkegaard, Teresa of Avila, St. Ignatius, and other masters of the spiritual life have written on these matters. This book attempts to put into contemporary language the experiences about which the spiritual masters wrote. The author respects and uses the data of psychology. The theories of Kierkegaard, Erikson, and St. Ignatius have helped him greatly in understanding the data he has discovered in his experience. He has found that the Holy Spirit has been operative in a person's life prior to his coming for spiritual guidance and that that same Spirit is leading the person forward in the ongoing process of spiritual growth and development. The person travels at one moment in many preceding and succeeding moments.

The present "moment" has a governing grace. The book describes the dynamic toward growth which operates in several different governing graces. Soren Kierkegaard speaks of three levels of lived experience: the instinctive level, the ethical level, and the religious level. The author has found this conceptualization helpful in understanding his experience of dealing with those who come to him for spiritual direction. He has found a significant difference between the first two levels and the third. The religious level involves the leap of faith. It also involves a dynamic of growth he believes the *Spiritual Exercises* of St. Ignatius help clarify. To a certain extent, he finds a correspondence between this spiritual dynamic and the psychosexual dynamic described in Erikson's epigenetic theory.

Chapters Six through Ten will delineate this correspondence and describe the developmental life of the person of faith.

This book treats the pattern of growth in a linear fashion, though in reality few people have such a neat progression. In general, the pattern of growth tends to be more cyclical where in later stages one goes back over previous stages of growth or incorporates one's previous advances in a new way. For the purposes of clarity, it seems best to the author to present a unilinear development. The seven passages of growth he will treat are: 1) belief in an impersonal God (or some inadequate notion of God); 2) belief in God as Creator; 3) belief in God as Savior; 4) belief in Jesus as human; 5) belief in Jesus as struggling to love; 6) belief in Jesus as loving through suffering; and 7) belief in the risen Jesus, the Holy Spirit, and the Church.

In his experience the author has had a number of people come to him for spiritual direction who really do not have a personal relationship with God. Chapters Two through Five, describe the process of growth for such persons and deal with the leap of faith as a person combats his negative or idealized self-image and finally says "yes" to the fact that God has created him good in His own image.

Chapters Six through Ten treat of explicit faith development, that is, of a life lived in conscious relationship with a personal God. Chapter Nine treats the same person traversing four successive passages of growth in discipleship and in relationship with Jesus.

All the stages of development involve a dying process which is much akin to the dying process that Elizabeth Kubler-Ross describes in her book *On Death and Dying*.[11] Each chapter

---

[11]Elizabeth Kubler-Ross, *On Death and Dying* (New York, 1969).

describes the letting go that happens as a person grows in faith to a new level and surrenders to grace.

Structure of the chapters

Each descriptive chapter strives to do four things: 1) portray the sense of self that the person has; 2) portray the person's sense of the world; 3) describe the person's experience of God and prayer; and 4) examine the nature of the choices for growth facing the person. Verbatims will be used as a way of making the experience concrete.[12] Three additional chapters describe how the spiritual director facilitates the process of growth at the different stages of development.

[12]Though the verbatims have been created by the author, they are not a-typical.

Part I
Inadequate Faith

2

BELIEF IN GOD AS LAWGIVER

Most of us strive to be good people. As youngsters, we were taught to obey the law. Yet one of the characteristics of maturity is the ability to step beyond the universal norm and apply it to a specific situation. The uniqueness of the situation may call for the person's "breaking" the law. Such an action often marks a significant step in a person's growth. Kohlberg's fifth level of moral development represents this step. The person goes beyond the accepted customs and norms of his society and recognizes that what may be right for him may not be right for others and vice versa. Often a person's growth summons him to go counter to his previous values in one of three very difficult areas: his family, his country, or his religion.

Breaking away from the laws of one's family may mean choosing a vocation or a spouse contrary to one's parents' wishes or other actions which go against their values. Many saw opposition to the war in Vietnam as unpatriotic, undermining our government and laws. Boycotts, civil rights protests, and opposition to the military-industrial complex were similarly categorized.

Some young fundamentalist Christians lead lives of smoking, dancing, and premarital sexual behavior. Many Catholics, too, have been making choices contrary to the explicit rules of the Church. Priests and religious have left their vowed life in order to marry; husbands and wives have separated and remarried. *Humanae Vitae*, with its prohibition of artificial means of birth control, pushed some Catholics to understand themselves, the magisterium, and the law of the Church in a whole new way which seemed to "transcend" the law.

Many view this behavior as regressive and sinful, as a move away from God's law, universal law, and discipline. Some would say that the fabric of human society has been destroyed. Many call for a return to principles—individually and socially. In most instances, the people involved experienced their choices as acts of courage founded upon a deeper faith and trust in the Lord. Their choices brought a peace and a security they had never known before, as well as embarrassment, disapproval from others, and a loss of accustomed support systems. They paid a heavy price to purchase what they experienced as freedom, truth, and love. They broke through barriers of sectarianism and narrow ethical and religious cultures; they entered a worldwide culture of unity with all human beings based on mutual tolerance and respect and the embrace of pluralistic society. Were they deceived? Or are we to understand their behavior in another way?

This chapter describes how a person lives a life of principle or a life at the moral-ethical level of Kierkegaard. In order to grow in faith, one must move from trusting abstract universal norms to embracing relationship.

We shall take the case of Phil, a twenty-nine-year-old, newly-ordained priest who has been assigned to a large suburban parish. He has just preached a Sunday homily and is discussing that homily with an older priest.

> Phil: Well, the homily yesterday really went well. I had prepared all week for it. The readings were about the Church; the Gospel was Matthew 16, so I had as my theme topic: the Church. As my theme sentence I had: "The Church perceives God's will as the higher ideal by which we Catholics are to live." I developed the notion that we all are the People of God, but that the Church institutionally has received the truth from God and passes that divine truth on to us. I explained the meaning of tradition. God is known through His Will and His Will is known through the way the Church teaches and speaks to us. I gave two examples of the difficulty of following God's will: one was a case of a married couple who no longer love each other but who stay together for the sake of their three children because of the commitment they made to one another and to God's Will at the time of their marriage; another was the case of a couple who had many burdens financially and much sickness, and I explained the call of God's Will to either abstain from sex or to practice rhythm. It seemed important to give some examples about the nature of the Church in the concrete; so that's why I talked about no divorce and no contraception.

> Older priest (feeling overwhelmed and wanting to be patient with this theology from the pulpit): So, you are pleased with the way you prepared your homily, the way you developed it, and the way it was received.

> Phil: Yes. I really was. And the people really heard what I said. After Mass there were a handful of men and women who came back to the sacristy to talk about it.

> Older priest: Oh?

Phil: Yes. They had really heard what I had said about God's Will and the teaching of the Church against birth control and divorce. A few of them were a bit upset. They wanted to know whether there were exceptions. Evidently one of them had a relative who was divorced and re-married and wanted to know why the Church could not accept her since her second marriage seemed to be such a good one. And they all complained about it being a serious sin to practice birth control. So I had an opportunity to explain to them how an individual's perception must give way to the Church's perception of the way things are because the Church's ideal—through the hierarchy—is higher than an individual's. I told them that it was a matter of God's Will for them and that they were to believe in all that the Church taught. I emphasized how they would grow spiritually as Catholics through their setting aside their own egocentric way, their desire to satisfy their own needs. I told them how as a priest I'd like to be able to say to them "If it feels good, it is good" because then they would like me. But I told them that I couldn't teach that way. We all have a cross to bear: that's my cross as a priest, and they have a cross as married people.

Older priest (feeling a bit angry that this young cleric was talking down to his parishioners): Well, Phil, you certainly came across rather strongly to them. Do you have any sense why they were upset?

Phil (pausing): Uh, I . . . I hadn't given it much thought. It just seemed that this was the right moment to tell them what God's Will for them really is and to call forth their faith. Ah . . . maybe they were feeling guilty. In fact, I wouldn't be surprised if (smiling) that one who spoke about her relative who had divorced and re-married wasn't speaking about herself. I didn't say this to her, but maybe she was being convicted for her own sins and that's why she came back to the sacristy.

Sense of Self

Phil is concerned about the truth, about doing right and avoiding wrong, about sin or doing what feels good. Words like "egocentricity," "selfishness," "higher ideal," all point to his sense of self. He does not know how to speak the truth compassionately or in a nuanced way. Instead he speaks from an ideal or an ideology. He thinks logically, and he prays logically—probably thinking about what is right and what is wrong. He has set aside his own judgment and given way to the Church's way of perceiving. What he has set aside is properly set aside; but somehow Jesus, the compassionate one, does not come through in Phil's homilies. The Church has helped this young man die to his own selfishness as it calls others to die to selfishness. However, he does not yet understand nor live the life of a mature adult which involves an intimate conversation with the Father or Jesus.

Phil wants people (himself included) to do the right thing. He focuses on behavior and the rules for behaving. He suspects that he really is idealistic. If he sins, he picks himself up and tries harder. As yet he knows nothing of being saved by the One who alone can save; he hopes for salvation from his own efforts to be the perfect priest. He experiences the cross as fidelity to the truth which he understands the Church to be demanding. He understands the Church as the people of God; but he sees the hierarchy, and not the people, as the point at which God is experienced, discerned, understood, and followed.

A person living a life of principle lacks a sense of his own uniqueness and that of others. Rather he judges that we are all of the same mold, that we all strive for the same perfection and the ideal. He operates with an idealized self-image. He relies almost exclusively on reason. He distrusts other levels of his personality—especially his feelings and emotions. Often he recognizes his feelings and emotions, but he considers them suspect and unreliable. As much as possible, he suppresses or represses them. Usually he will develop habits for coping with strong feelings. He may debunk affectivity and intimacy as sentimentality. He combats passion and sexual feelings with vigorous plans—distracting self with various activities or praying that the "temptation" (feelings and impulses) will go away. He judges all affection as dangerous because it could lead to breaking the law. Suppression or repression is effective for some, though eventually there may occur a crisis where the feelings burst forth, often in a "messy" way. Distractions, too, can be effective for a time; but the person feels in continual tension and generally grows weary of the struggle. Some people judge that they are sinners in this process, and repentance flows from their sense of failure.

The person of principle thinks that reason will triumph over emotions and impulses. Hence, he makes tremendous efforts at control. He judges that he can solve all "problems" at the level of understanding and that his will can overcome all obstacles. He develops various habits, virtues, and customs for they bring safety. Good habits and solid virtues bring security and protection from the unknown, the unresolved and the unexperienced. Good habits lead to efficiency, to productivity, and to achievement of goals. Virtue leads ultimately to the striving for perfection, which is the highest goal. One reaches perfection following God's Will.

A person of principle believes in a universal law or ideal for all. By effort and in time, all of us can attain the ideal which embraces the greatest good and the universal norm for behavior. A reward awaits those who strive to attain this universal law by doing good and avoiding evil; punishment threatens those who disregard or fail to strive to attain this universal law.

The person of principle focuses a great deal on the price to be paid in life. He accepts suffering as part of life—not the suffering that occurs in interpersonal relationships (which he generally suppresses), but rather the suffering that comes from the awareness of physical evil in the world. He strives to change physical evil; it is the effort and not the outcome that matters.

The person of principle has an inflated sense of responsiblity for his actions. He struggles to live up to his own ideals and to others' expectations of him (or what he thinks they expect of him). He wants to earn salvation. Frequently, he recognizes his actions as good; yet he deeply needs the approval of others since he does not yet have a unique sense of self. He depends heavily on external norms and customs and demands much of himself. He also demands much of others and expects them to live up to universal law expressed in God's will.

Sense of the World

The person of principle believes that all should do good and avoid evil. He applies the same norm to the world that he applies to himself: one must live up to and fulfill his obligations. He relates to others out of a sense of duty. Ordinarily, the person of principle does not have a large perspective. Generally, his largest sense of "world" is his country. If one were to use Kohlberg's classifications of people in terms of moral behavior, the person of principle includes those people in Stages Four through Six. Kohlberg classifies most people in Stage Four, where one's loyalty and sense of direction come from a larger group, usually one's country. Thus, many persons of principle focus on issues of national pride and honor and take necessary steps to preserve patriotism.

Some persons of principle move beyond loyalty to one's own country and pride in one's nation to a large global sense. These persons possess a more universal sense of justice and may focus on such issues as human rights, equal opportunity, equality of distribution of goods, and punishment for those nations and corporations that take more than their due.

All these people are motivated by an ideal which *must* or *should* be achieved. Frequently, they are dedicated to some cause. Obviously, such a movement is quite good. At this point in growth, they experience a call to set right that which is wrong and to choose fidelity to the good. They are moving from self-centeredness and licentiousness toward a more universal sense of rightness.

Not infrequently they become intolerant of those who break the law and desire to impose penalties for failing to live up to the ideal. Many Americans reacted indignantly to the peace movement during the Vietnam War because it called our government into question. "Hard hats" marched furiously in New York after the Cambodian invasion. Slogans such as, "Love it or leave it," flag decals for cars, and the Nixon campaign slogan "Law and Order" held sway.

The same type of motivation operates within the Roman Catholic Church in such organizations as Catholics United for the Faith (CUF) which tries to negate the renewal of Vatican II. These Catholics prefer the security of the Church they knew prior to 1960 and obedience to its laws. Groups motivated by principles impose penalties on those who do not show loyalty to the organization, e.g., imprisonment for draft resisters or conscientious objectors and ex-communications for the divorced. They use fear and force to achieve the ideals they hold. Generally, guilt overtakes the person who desires to remain in the group but cannot abide by all its laws. For example, a person feels unpatriotic even in criticizing his nation or calling for prison reform or a cutback in military expenditures. Within the Roman Catholic Church, persons using artificial means of birth control choose to abstain from Communion or not even to attend Mass. They are unable to nuance the law which they consider absolute; one who breaks the law, no matter what the reasons or circumstances, is guilty and should be punished.

The dialogue narrated above between Phil and the older priest does not give us a sense of Phil's world view. In most circumstances he would choose loyalty to his country. When that loyalty conflicts with his loyalty to the Church, he would choose loyalty to the Church.

Experience of God and prayer

The person of principle imagines God as a transcendent Judge who has given the universal law which guides his life. Though he considers God as personal, he experiences Him as remote. God asks him to make an effort; and, when he fails, God helps him pick himself up and try again. God gives him the grace to live up to His (his own) ideals and to become perfect by overcoming his sin and sinful tendencies.

God is most concerned with his actions: the good he does and the evil he avoids. He knows his behavior and keeps a record of his actions. He will reward him with eternal life if he keeps His commandments and precepts; He will punish him with damnation or purgatory if he fails to keep them.

Most people of principle focus on sexuality and anger as their primary sins. They generally experience God only through fear, afraid lest God, who is the Judge of evil, will punish them with eternal damnation. Because they admire Jesus and His sacrifice, they are capable of a great deal of self-sacrifice. The person of principle may have a sense of God's providence; and, in difficult times, he generally trusts that God will help him. Often he has the knowledge that God is a good Father or gentle and loving, but generally he does not feel that goodness or love. He grasps God intellectually, not experientially.

Let us pick up again the conversation between Phil and his pastor. The older priest has been taken aback at Phil's lack of compassion for the woman who had come back to the sacristy and tries to open up the experience of a compassionate Jesus for Phil. The dialogue continues.

> Older priest: Well, Phil, I'd suggest that you take her to God in prayer this week and ask Him about the homily you gave and the way you delivered it.

> Phil: Oh, I did pray over the readings all this last week. That's how come I gave the homily the way I did.

> Older priest (surprised and wondering): How did you go about praying?

Phil: Well, the way I normally pray. I understand that prayer is tuning oneself into God's presence and His Word, turning one's thoughts to God and to the awareness of His Will. So, I took the commentary on Matthew and took notes on it and then I read through my notes from my Moral Theology classes and thought about God's teaching and how His people need to hear the truth which the Church communicates from God.

Older priest: I see. Well, maybe tomorrow when you pray, you might remember the look on that woman's face and ask Jesus how he regards her, how He feels for her, and whether He accepts her. I also encourage you to pray over the readings for next Sunday. Talk to the Father and to Jesus personally, like a friend. How does that sound?

Phil: Well, I'll try. I don't know what that means to talk friend to friend with God. I mean, I really respect God and want to do His Will. And I accept all that the Church teaches us to believe about God. Didn't I pray the right way? Did I do something wrong? I only told them what we were taught in the seminary. Did I make a mistake? I know that some of the profs at the sem told me that I was too idealistic, but I've been working on that. (pausing and thinking) I *will* pray harder and work harder on next Sunday's homily.

Older priest: Okay, Phil. Just remember that you too are like those people out there to whom you are preaching and that you're like that woman who came back to the sacristy.

Phil (laughing as he leaves): Oh, my supervisor is telling me not to preach down to them again.

Generally, the person of principle uses discursive meditation as his form of prayer. He applies the principles of scripture to his own personal life so as to have greater conformity to the Will of God. He frequently has many good insights. We see this pattern in Phil. The text of Matthew on divorce does not apply to him personally, but it does apply to married couples. He interprets it just as rigidly for them as he would if it applied to himself.

Phil focuses upon the text as a problem for his listeners to solve—which is the way he prays himself. Most people leading lives of principle preoccupy themselves with problems in prayer: overcoming a temptation, resolving a painful relationship, enduring a frustrating or unsatisfying occupation. Frequently they examine their conscience: where have I failed? how can I do better in the future? someday I may reach the state of perfection. They seldom focus on the Lord; generally, they focus on self and their failures. They strive to imitate Jesus—especially Jesus on the cross. Jesus suffered and died; so I ought not to run away from suffering in my life but should accept my cross just the way my Savior accepted His. Often people of principle are led to hope for the reward of life everlasting rather than to experience any joy here and now.

In the instance of the homily, Phil has been doing for others exactly what he does for himself: he has been imposing standards and asking others to measure up to them. In all innocence, he uses the Church, God's Will, and Scripture as a universal norm which calls for fidelity and self-sacrifice. Though he does not explicitly state this, he imagines God as a Lawgiver and Judge—both for himself and for the people. The older priest, in the wisdom of his experience, tries gently to indicate that Jesus may be other than Phil imagines. Phil moves into self-doubt and resolves to try harder the next time.

Phil and the older priest engage in "spiritual conversation," i.e., discussion about God and the things associated with God and religion. The person of principle ordinarily approaches his own personal growth indirectly. He often seeks to talk about problems or discuss understandings and theological questions with an older person who is more experienced. He approaches the question as a general principle which can be applied universally rather than as something which can be applied uniquely and personally to himself or to others. He may use confession, admitting some failure to live up to a universal norm. Spiritual conversation is different from spiritual direction where the director appreciates the unique inner movements of the individual precisely as unique to the individual.

Passage to growth

Once the person of principle has internalized the law and developed good habits, he may continue for some time striving to prove his own worth. When his weakness surfaces, he struggles to conquer it. He constantly focuses on his behavior—sometimes for years—until he experiences something traumatic or until he gradually becomes dissatisfied with himself and his life.

Often the person of principle moves to a new level of growth through some traumatic happening in the area of interpersonal relationships. His feelings become so strong that he can no longer control them and thus must deal with them. The traumatic event may be sexual infidelity to celibacy or marriage, the death of a parent or child, serious sickness in one's own life or family, or failure in one's job. Usually the person experiences negative feelings, such as anger, sorrow or guilt. He feels punished beyond what he deserves. After all, since he has been striving hard to be good, how can God let this happen to him? He may be tempted to shortcircuit the experience, often through confession. Though the traumatic experience often surfaces strong negative feelings, one can also experience positive ones, such as love or wonder. Occasions such as falling in love or the birth of a child may trigger these feelings.

A traumatic event is not a necessary precondition. Sometimes a person grows suspicious that there is something more to life than just striving to fulfill the law. The person of principle begins to ask the question: Is that all there is? He knows that he has striven to be good, has done many charitable things for others, can be quite self-sacrificing, and can live in much hope with deep forbearance. But he misses a sense of joy and freedom in his life. He begins to question the principle of rationality which has ruled his life and may begin to experiment with alternative forms of behavior. Generally feelings, and actions that flow from them, open the door to new growth.

Let us turn again to Phil and the older priest. Four years have elapsed; both have matured. Phil works at another parish and has been praying regularly for two years; the older priest has studied to be a spritual director since a number of younger priests come to him for "spiritual direction." Phil has begun to keep a spiritual journal and has now made a personally directed retreat. Phil still focuses a good deal on problems, but he comes monthly to talk about his life with the older priest.

> Phil: I'm really grateful that we could get together today, and yet I am also very anxious. There's a topic that I've not talked about except in confession.

Older priest: (a caring, receptive look)

Phil: Ah, I, uh, don't know how to begin. Uh, (coughing) my sinus must be acting up. Ah, it's about my sexuality and, I'm been having problems, as you know, with masturbation and impure thoughts. Well, what's really got me scared is that this young woman whom I've been counseling, well, I've been thinking of her whenever I'm not doing something active and (looking down) I've been struggling. So I've kept busy. My pastor calls me a workaholic; if only he knew why. Well, the reason why I'm so upset is that I feel like I've been fighting a losing battle with all these thoughts about this woman, and now, last week-end, when she was saying good-bye after our conference, (pausing) I don't know what happened to me. I lost control. (long pause, looks at director)

Older priest (in steady tone): So, you lost control.

Phil: Yes, I lost control and I've felt out of control ever since. I think I'm in love. I'm a priest . . . and I'm in love. How could God do this to me? How come He didn't protect me? How could He? I've given myself to Him and He's let me fall in love. I can't get her off my mind. (long pause) I could laugh and cry at the same time. I've been praying to become a more loving priest, but I didn't mean this kind of love.

Older priest: You're pretty upset with God.

Phil: And I'm pretty upset with Ginny (that's the woman). It's her fault too for starting all this. If she hadn't kissed me and held me, it wouldn't have happened. I wonder maybe I should never see her again. Yet I do care for her and I still want to be a priest. I don't know what to do. What should I do? (pleading) Tell me what to do. I'm so confused!

Older priest: I do sense that you are confused and angry at God and Ginny and maybe even at yourself for feeling the way you feel and for losing control.

Phil: Hey, I mean nothing all that serious happened. I kissed her back and held her for about ten seconds. That's all that happened. She's so good, so lovable and so loving toward me. I am confused and I'm really upset. I have all these feelings for her. I'm afraid of what I might do or where this might lead.

Older priest: You've a lot of feelings and thoughts. I wonder if you've shared these with the Lord.

Phil: I feel that He's abandoned me. He won't answer me. All I get from Him is: "Trust, I'm Your God." And Ginny, well, I feel like talking all this out with her and telling her what she's doing to me and that I really do want to be a celibate priest and that I need her help.

Older priest: Well?

Phil: Well, I'm afraid. It's too risky. I'm defenseless before her. What if she takes advantage of me? What if one thing leads to another? She's such a warm person; I've seen her with her sisters and brothers. The funny thing is, she's been thinking about entering religious life; so I've been meeting with her to help her make a decision about that. I don't want to mess up her life or my own.

Older priest: So, on the one hand, you'd like to talk all this out with Ginny; but, on the other hand, you are afraid to trust her with what is going on inside you. And when you've turned to the Lord, He invites you to trust. It seems that you don't as yet know what the Lord wants you to do about talking with Ginny. At least, you're not certain. Maybe you need to talk this out with Him first and then, depending on what happens in your prayer, either talk with Ginny or wait.

Phil: But tell me what I should do. I don't want to make a mistake. I want to be a celibate priest and faithful to the Lord and I also want to talk this out with Ginny.

Older priest: Can you bring both these "wants" of yours and entrust your whole self to the Lord? You'll know what to do in time. I encourage you to face Him.

We see here the struggle of Phil. He has striven to be faithful to the law and a good and generous priest. As he has encountered others more deeply, he has become more human and understanding. Now he senses himself falling in love and is confused because he really desires priesthood. He cannot deny his feelings. He senses the goodness of Ginny and his attraction to her. He judges this as inconsistent with whom he senses himself to be (a celibate priest) and whom he has known the Lord to be (Lawgiver). A new image of God is emerging as the One who calls to trust, but thus far Phil only feels abandoned by God. He does not *understand* this God who calls him to trust. To grow he will have to let go his need to understand and enter into mystery.

The person of principle deeply desires to conform himself to God and His Will. Gradually his desires will lead to a threatening intimacy which opens the door to union with a personal and living God. As the person begins to experience this personal, living God, he senses his own uniqueness which is beyond conformity to the divine law and doing good deeds. He begins to open to his own interiority and inner experience.

Forces of resistance and forces of attraction exert themselves. Negatively, defenses against the call to growth arise. The person may belittle his call to growth. He may speak cynically about relationships and intimacy, about subjectivity, about feelings, impulses, and affections in general. The person of principle uses his greatest gift—the universalizing of insights—to form another generalization: All those who move beyond the intellect into the realm of feelings are psychologizing religious experience and making a god of psychology or feelings. When anger or resentment surfaces, the person will be tempted to suppress his feelings rather than to explore them. If sexual feelings arise, the person may run from them and miss the intimacy to which he is called. Phil desires to run from his feelings. He knows he has feelings of sexual attraction for Ginny; yet he fears owning them—especially with Ginny—for fear of what might happen. He fears losing control. He is not sure that he can trust Ginny or himself or even the Lord.

Various forces aid the person in the process of moving through this passage to a new level of growth, most especially, the call to trust the Lord in a deeper way. As the Lord implants this call in Phil, Phil only feels more abandoned. If the spiritual director encourages Phil to stay with his feelings and experience, Phil may gradually begin to listen to this call to trust the Lord. Initially, this call to trust is more cognitive than affective. Gradually, Phil will get in touch with something deeper within himself—something which is yet unnamed and unclaimed. He wants to be more free and more human. The Lord beckons Phil to new growth through these desires. He is urging Phil to step beyond his security in the law and to entrust himself and his future to Him. The desire for greater union with the Lord and His people, the yearning for closeness in and with Jesus, leads the person of principle to make a new leap of faith.

The person of principle generally "dies a slow death" in the process of becoming a unique person in relationship with the Lord and others. Usually, he goes on a long time denying the need for any change. He clings to the security gained through living the right principles and thinks that he does well. When things go awry, he strives to find the right principle to correct them.

When he experiences his inability to correct something or when the pain becomes too strong, he will deeply sense the need for change. If the process has been gradual, he may discover his need when an individual friend or a community challenges him to recognize that something in his life is awry, missing, unnamed, or unclaimed. He will struggle for a time to discover what he can do to win back others' approval, but all efforts will be in vain. He may move to anger at others' inconsistencies, trying to justify his resistance to growth and change.

If he experiences powerlessness through some traumatic event, he will generally direct his anger at God. How can God allow this to happen to him when he has been so faithful? If God were really good, He would not have allowed this to happen, or He would cure him of his anger and powerlessness.

Phil knows that he did not want to happen what has happened. Therefore, he finds it difficult to claim responsibility for the situation. He has blamed both God and Ginny. Blaming others or God for one's situation may take only a brief time or may extend over a long period. In the end, it proves fruitless; the person remains powerless. As the person of principle becomes more anxious and desirous of winning back approval, he begins to compromise. He may acknowledge some feelings: anger, hatred, love, sexual feelings. He may risk being transparent and vulnerable in some relationship. He may let go some security or law, risking punishment or loss of control. Thus, most probably, Phil will hesitatingly choose to reveal his inner feelings to Ginny. In risking this revelation, he will feel most vulnerable; but as he shares his true feelings and becomes more intimate with Ginny, he will discover that he likes what is happening and that he even feels freer in his ministry with others.

Often the deepest wrestling will center around the enjoyment he experiences in being with Ginny. He considers this enjoyment as a sign of his selfishness. When the person living a life of principle has tasted some of his own uniqueness and has gotten in touch with some of his deeper desires, he fears being selfish. He felt secure and safe as long as he did "what God wanted," as long as he obeyed the law. God does not cater to our "whims," but asks fidelity to the law. When he denied himself and suppressed his feelings and desires, he felt united with Jesus on the cross and felt he was ascending the pathway to heaven.

But now Phil wonders whether he is indeed on that pathway any more. He likes himself more and feels more spontaneous; he finds his ministry and preaching more real. He no longer preaches down to the people. Since he sees himself as sinful, weak, and confused, how can he judge others? But despite the positive growth that he sees in himself, he feels unsure.

The challenge before the person of principle is to let go of all that he has known before, to let go of his ideals and the security he has felt in trying to keep the law. God calls him to trust wherever He might lead and to trust his deepest desires as the place of God's revelation. God calls him to risk, which evokes radical change at the core of his being. He cannot compromise. If he wants freedom, he has to let go of his "old self." He has dedicated his life to principles, but has failed to integrate his principles with his feelings. When, at last, he turns his anger against himself and becomes depressed and filled with self-pity, he feels sad and powerless. He does not know how to change or allow himself to come alive. He does not know how to change the old habits. He does not know how to surrender to a loving Lord. His fears paralyze him.

Let us return to the situation of Phil. After being faithful to spiritual direction and journal-keeping for about three years, he has gradually drifted away from both practices. He had not seen the older priest for about a year when they met at a funeral. Phil took the initiative and said, "I ought to see you." They arranged to get together a week later.

> (Phil enters. His shoulders are slumped; his face and eyes are without life. He keeps looking at the floor rather than at the older priest. His voice is a monotone. He says little. Finally, the older priest begins to take more initiative.)
>
> Older priest (sympathetically): You're having a pretty rough time.
>
> Phil: Terrible.
>
> Older priest: Do you want to talk about it?
>
> Phil: Not really. But it's horrible. (Long silence. Phil stares at the floor.) He sputters hesitantly: I haven't seen you for a long time. I don't know what to do. I feel paralyzed. I'm ashamed of myself—and yet I'm not. I'm so confused. I feel torn. I wish I were dead. (Pause.) I guess I ought to explain.
>
> The older priest looks respectively and compassionately, but says nothing.

Phil: Well, that girl I talked to you about—Ginny—she and I have been seeing an awful lot of each other. I can't explain it, but I've never become so close. We've done a lot of things I guess we shouldn't have done. (A long pause. The older priest looks compassionately, but says nothing.) I don't know who I am anymore. I want to be a priest, but I also want to be with Ginny. (Again a long pause.) I never realized I had such strong feelings, but I do. (Another long pause. Phil appears pensive and pained.) I don't know how God puts up with me. I wish He'd change me. It's amazing. I've been spending time with Him every morning, but He hasn't said anything to me in a long time. I really do love Ginny, and yet I think I want to be a priest. I don't think I should be feeling the way I do.

Older priest: But you are.

Phil (after a long pause): If only it were O.K. . . .

Older priest: It isn't O.K.?

Phil: Well, it doesn't make sense. I think what I'm doing is wrong. Yet, deep down, it seems right. My head can't make sense of it.

Older priest: And yet it seems right at the depths of your being?

Phil (hesitantly): Yes. And I'm not able to change what's at the depths of my being. And I can't deny it. When I've tried to do either, I've gotten sick physically or withdrawn from people and ministry. That's what went on all last fall.

Older priest: So you can't deny it, and you can't change. You're powerless right now.

Phil: Yes, that's right; I'm powerless.

Older priest: And where is God in your powerlessness?

Phil: I don't know where God is. I wonder if He's given up on me.

Older priest: So you think God's given up on you.

Phil: No. I know He doesn't give up on anybody.

Older priest: So He's not given up on you.

Phil: No, but I don't know how He puts up with me.

Older priest: You mean He puts up with you?

Phil: Sure. He's more tolerant of me than I am of myself.

Older priest: So God's accepting of who you are and where you are now. He's affirming what is going on deep within you—the desires and the powerlessness.

Phil: Yes, but funny I never thought about it that way. But yes.

Older priest: Maybe it's appropriate that you just dwell in God's acceptance of you now.

The person of principle experiences freedom when he allows someone to love him in the paralysis. The change to which he is called involves accepting his present reality, owning it before others and the Lord, listening to their acceptance, and believing these things. In doing so, he begins to trust his own uniqueness as a self, his own feelings, and his deepest desires. He knows deeply his own needs for love and that love is offered no matter what his experience or feelings. He accepts the call to be in relationship without pretense and to share his feelings and desires no matter what they are. Phil's openness with Ginny had been leading him to deeper intimacy with her and greater acceptance of himself. Now the older priest calls Phil to be open and intimate with the Lord. He urges Phil to bring his real person before the Lord and to listen to the Lord's love and acceptance. Phil knows that he can no longer control life's circumstances through living his principles. He is beginning to accept the gift quality of life and of himself. The more he lets go of his need to save himself, the more he will experience his own uniqueness.

Summary

We have described a process of growth as a person begins to claim his own identity uniquely before the Lord. The person lets go of his reliance on universal principles which he has applied to all situations and begins to rely on the Lord who loves the person uniquely in specific circimstances. He moves from Kierkegaard's moral-ethical level to the level of religious faith. The person realizes the futility of striving to keep the universal law perfectly and the futility of always striving to control one's own and others' behavior through observance of the law. He lets go of the ideal image of the self and accepts the specificity of his own and others' uniqueness.

In practice, the person often breaks the law which he had once cherished and found helpful. He commits this "sin" with trepidation, but without guilt. Many adults have never taken this risk which opens the door to a new personal relationship with God. This passage is the first significant passage that one passes through in one's spiritual quest. It opens the door to a felt life of faith and belief in a personal God.

3

BELIEF IN GOD AS GIVER OF PLEASURE

The author began his reflections on spiritual growth thinking that the *Spiritual Exercises* of St. Ignatius provided a valid prism through which he could view religious experience. As he engaged in ministry, however, he discovered many who were not yet ready for the *Spiritual Exercises*, many who had not yet owned that they were uniquely and personally loved by God. Though these people had lived in religious life or the seminary—some for many years—and though they may have been faithful to a time for prayer for much of that time, still many had not experienced God personally. They were moving on the path toward religious experience, but had not yet had the experience. As he did spiritual direction, he discovered two paths to personal relationship with God—the path of whim and the path of reason. These paths correspond in some way to the instinctive and the moral-ethical levels of Soren Kierkegaard. In dealing with older people who were striving to express religious commitment, he found many more on the path of reason than on the path of whim, yet he did discover some on the path of whim. It seems good to describe this person and how he or she relates to God and grows in freedom. In the previous chapter, the author described the person of principle who leads his life by reason.

Generally, people of whim are younger people; however, some older people have never really developed and others have reverted to earlier stages. We will follow the story of Teresa, a thirty-nine-year-old married woman who has come to make her first personally directed retreat. She is quite attractive and fashionably dressed, with the two top buttons of her blouse unbuttoned. She sports a pleasant cologne. A layman, Bill, is the person assigned as her retreat director. We begin with the opening conference.

Bill: Well, hello, Teresa. How are you?

Teresa: Well, I don't know. This is all so new to me. I've never made a directed retreat before. What do I do?

Bill: Well, usually on the first day of a retreat, the first time we get together, I like to spend a little time having the person talk about herself, where she's from, how she's gotten to the point she's at, and why she's come to make this retreat. I also usually talk a bit about myself. This is your first directed retreat, then?

Teresa: Yes, it is. (crossing her legs in such a way that they are more exposed) I was surprised not to have a priest. Do you work out here a lot?

Bill: I've been here on a part-time basis for the last ten years. So you're surprised not to have a priest?

Teresa: It's okay with me. I'm not mad. I'm from Pennsylvania. I heard this was a really good place. I've never made this kind of retreat before. I'm married and have two children; no, three children. My husband is the vice-president of Christenson Airlines. It's a good business. He set it up. What else can I say about myself? I'm thirty-nine-years-old. I'm very active in my parish. I didn't used to be. But it's more and more fun for me to be in the parish. I'm not as busy as I used to be.

Bill: So you have some time available. How old are your children?

Teresa (pausing as she lights up a cigarette): Bobby's the youngest. He's brain-damaged. He's been in a home since he was six months old. I don't see him very much. My next is fifteen years old and the oldest is a freshman in college.

Bill: So one child is away in school and another is brain-damaged in a home.

Teresa: We didn't expect a handicapped child. When he was born, we decided we couldn't care for him at home and that he needed a place where he could be cared for. We just couldn't care for him at home.

Bill: It would take too much time and energy.

Teresa: It wouldn't be doing him any good. His birth was such a disappointment. I don't know why God does such things. The best thing seemed to be to have him institutionalized. It's pretty awful. It'd be depressing for me to take care of a child that would never get better.

Bill: So you felt disappointed at his birth.

Teresa: Yes, it was awful. It really was the turning point in my life. We were surprised by my pregnancy, but it was a nice surprise. So when he was born, it was such a shock. It was so awful. It just confused everything. I have to tell you some things about my family.

Sense of Self

The person of whim measures experience through his feelings—generally, surface feelings. Feelings of fun, pleasure, immediate gratification, and satiation provide the norm for behavior. These feelings control the person's life. When he feels good, he *is* good; what feels good *is* good. When he feels bad, he *is* bad; what feels bad *is* bad.

Very often the person of whim appears flighty and seems unable to stick to the point. The person also has difficulty communicating much about self. Thus Teresa expresses interest in the fact that the director is a layman and talks more about her family than she does about herself.

The person of whim often exudes sensuality. The rush of emotions and affections characterize the person of whim—the delight at being with friends or having fun, the pleasure of food or drink or sex, the experience of being "turned on," the thrill of competition. Not infrequently feelings lead to a satiation which in turn becomes addiction: addiction to food, to drink (beer, wine, alcohol), to sex (promiscuity), to drugs, or to gambling. As Bill will eventually discover, Teresa is more or less "addicted" to working in her parish. In this section of the conference she refers to her service as "fun." To some extent, she is also looking for a "high" on this retreat.

The person of whim generally values the body, the experience of touch, and how he looks and smells. The body often becomes another norm for life. Many persons of whim focus in an exaggerated way on their bodies: being alluring in clothes, slimness, hair, perfume, colors. Some indulge in an excessive use of creaturely comforts. All of them live by developing what feels good and by avoiding what feels bad.

The person of whim can be quite materialistic. To have more is to be more; to have more pleasure is to be more alive. To satisfy one's body-desires is to be more one's self. Our American culture with its advertising appeals to the person of whim. "Buy, procure, use" exemplify typical attitudes. Clothes, an attractive woman or man, a sporting car, toilet articles, etc., make a person lovable. Fashion, styles, and trends provide a norm for choice. "Freedom" happens when one buys the right product. Teresa exhibits her materialism in her dress and in her concern for her looks. Later in the conference she will manifest her appreciation for the good things that her husband's job provides.

The person of whim looks upon himself as the center of the universe. In general, Teresa does not reflect on the consequences that her behavior has on others. Though she speaks of her decision to put Bobby in a home as a decision for his good, we can see how much her own feelings enter this decision. She speaks of being with him as awful and depressing.

Just as it is characteristic of the person of whim to seek pleasure, it is perhaps even more characteristic of the person of whim to seek to avoid pain. Teresa presents a good example of this. She tries to blot Bobby out of her mind—even confusing the number of children that she has. She seldom visits him.

Sense of the world

The person of whim generally does not embrace a very large portion of the universe, since he himself has become the center of his universe. One might expect, at least, that Teresa would exhibit genuine concern for her handicapped child; but, even though she voices a concern for him, one gets the impression that she is really only concerned about escaping the pain that he brings her.

Since the person of whim keeps trying to avoid pain, he has practically no sense of justice and compassion. Below is an excerpt from the end of the initial conference where Teresa briefly expresses her fears.

> Teresa: I wanted to ask you one thing. You know the group meeting we had at the beginning. I got mad when the priest talked about nuclear disarmament. I saw your books. Does this place have a communist tendency? I have nightmares when I think about a nuclear holocaust. I don't want that shoved down my throat.
>
> Bill: Would you like to talk about it?
>
> Teresa: I don't want to talk about it. We can't do anything about it. I don't want to think about it.
>
> Bill: There's a lot you would like to avoid.
>
> Teresa (eyes staring at floor, hands fidgeting): Yes.
>
> Bill: We don't have to talk about it. But it upsets you. Maybe we could talk if you become upset.
>
> Teresa (continuing to stare at the floor): I'd rather not.

A chance remark in the opening session and the presence in the retreat house library of books concerning justice have elicited a strong response from Teresa. She has touched some of her deeper fears. Rather than face them, she seeks to avoid them. The person of whim continually seeks what is pleasurable and avoids what is painful.

Experience of God and prayer

The person of whim generally views God as the one who rewards him if he is good and the one who punishes him if he is bad. Some people of whim, who feel very out of control as their following of whims leads them into pain, imagine God as somehow controlling their life. They call upon Him in times of trouble. They generally "bargain" in their prayer, focusing upon external results. "God, please give me this." They use God for their own self-satisfaction.

Other people of whim have no awareness or experience of God. Though they may not explicitly deny the existence of God, they may have little or no sense of the transcendent reality of life. They experience only what is immediate and at hand; they value only the present moment. Thus, indulgence in the moment becomes a "god" they serve.

Even if the person of whim avows belief in God, he may exhibit a practical atheism. In this instance, his belief in God tends to be a deism. He considers God as uninvolved in this world and in his actions, aloof and impersonal. God set the world in motion, but lets us do whatever we want.

Not uncommonly, the person of whim makes no attempt to pray since God seems irrelevant. If the external factors of his life situation call for prayer, e.g., if he lives in the seminary or religious life, the person will make attempts to pray but will find it frustrating. God seems so distant. Often the person of whim says he wants to draw nearer to God or will voice a conviction that God is personal. But these are empty words without real meaning. God exists, but the person of whim does not find Him in a meaningful way. The person of whim does not know how to bring about a satisfying relationship with God, just as he does not know how to develop satisfying and mature interpersonal relationships nor does he know how to be his true self. A shallowness about self and others indicates a shallowness about God. Although the person of whim may be a teen-ager or a person in his fifth decade of life, he misunderstands the nature of God. He is ignorant that God is a person and hence unreceiving of God's personal love for him, even though he may exert much effort in and around the idea of God. He may even try to dialogue with God, but the connection or union never quite happens. The person of whim often tries new things and shifts his stance as he tries to relate to the Lord.

When struggling to pray, the person of whim reflects a good deal upon himself. This reflection on self usually leads to a certain ambivalence and restlessness. The person desires freedom and senses that things could be different, but he cannot distinguish his own spontaneous responses to immediate stimuli from a deeper sense of freedom which will take some discipline. Thus the person fears putting the necessary restrictions for freedom upon himself lest these restrictions curb his freedom. There results confusion and lack of hope. The person remains oblivious to the deeper issues of life. While knowing that he has little self-knowledge and almost no self-appropriation, the person deeply desires self-awareness and self-possession. Yet he may not act on these desires for lack of discipline.

Some people become persons of whim after a frustrating attempt to observe the law. As we saw in the previous chapter, the person of principle grows in faith and in personhood through becoming more spontaneous and trusting of the deeper movements within him. When the person of principle reverts to the person of whim rather than moving forward, he yields to his superficial movements (fear of pain and desire for pleasure) rather than to more substantial values. This movement is more typical of older persons of whim like Teresa. Let us continue with the conference as she begins to speak about her early life with her parents.

> Teresa: . . . I have to tell you something about my family. I grew up in one of these strict Catholic families. I mean, really strict. I don't think they exist any more. My father and mother went to Mass every morning. We had rosary at home every day. We went to Communion on the first Fridays. I was raised a good Catholic. I did everything right. I went to Catholic school. (pausing) Birth control has been a hard thing. It almost broke up our marriage. I stuck by it because the Church said so. I figured that the birth of Bobby was a message to us. You have to be responsible and careful, and there are laws that have to be broken. Then I felt guilty, that God was paying us back. I got real depressed after the baby was born.
>
> Bill: So you were a faithful Catholic.
>
> Teresa: Yes, I followed all the laws.
>
> Bill: But then, after the baby was born, you wondered how important it was to follow all these rules.
>
> Teresa: Yes. And I wondered if God was punishing me.
>
> Bill: Did you have a sense of why you felt God was punishing you?
>
> Teresa: I'm not sure.
>
> Bill: Did you feel that you had done something wrong?

Teresa: I guess I feel that, when something bad happens, there has to be a reason. My husband and I decided a couple years before this baby's birth that we weren't going to follow the birth control rule any more.

Bill: So, it's like God was punishing you for breaking the rule.

Teresa: Yes. I don't feel that way too much any more though, because I got real angry and then I got depressed and felt guilty. (pause; a deep sigh) There's this really great priest in our parish. We met regularly. It was so good to talk with him. My husband is so busy with the airlines, and Jim's not much into religion. He's a Catholic, but not like I was. The priest convinced me that the baby was not my fault. That encouraged me. That's why I don't pay too much attention to him. If I saw him, I would get depressed and feel guilty. I can't think much about him.

Bill: It always causes too much pain.

Teresa: Yes. It's awful. And I can't do anything about it anyway. The priest was very helpful.

We see in Teresa vestiges of the person of principle. She obeyed the laws of the Church because the Church said so. It could well be that she obeyed the laws for fear of punishment. When finally her marriage was having some difficulties, she decided to break the law by using artificial means of birth control. When, in spite of this, she gives birth to a handicapped child, she feels guilty and assumes God is punishing her.

Now that Teresa has come on retreat, the director hopes that she will have an experience of God which will alter her previous images of God as Punisher and of God as Giver of Pleasure. Bill hopes that she will meet God as a Person who loves her as she is. Let us continue with the conference to see how Bill begins to introduce this notion.

Teresa: ... the priest was very helpful. He's the one who suggested I come on this retreat.

Bill: So the priest helped you to move out of your anger and depression. How do you feel about him?

Teresa: I know he's really important to me.

Bill: So much so that you came on this retreat.

Teresa: He thought it would be helpful to me. I don't know why. He thought I'd enjoy it. I think everyone is so nice and friendly here. It'll be an interesting experience. I'll enjoy it. It's a beautiful place. It's good to be away for a while.

Bill: But why did *you*, *Teresa*, want to come? You say you came to get a sense of peace and to please your parish priest.

Teresa: I just thought I'd enjoy it.

Bill: So you're hoping for a high experience. Often we need to spend time seeing what we're like. You do a lot of things; now is a time to *be*. It's a different way of relating to the Lord. What is it that you want from the Lord? Can you spend some time reflecting on why you said "yes" to coming here?

Teresa: I'm so glad the weather is nice. I saw the lawn chairs. I'm hoping to keep my tan going. I brought some books and a set of tapes. I want to see if they are as good as people say they are.

Bill: I wonder if you might just set aside a certain amount of time for that during the day like from 2:00 to 4:00 p.m.

Teresa: You mean make a schedule!

Bill: Well, I was thinking you might do some reading, but that you would also spend some time reflecting on what you are hoping for from the Lord. What does Teresa really want? If the

Lord were sitting in this chair, what would you say to Him?

Teresa: That would be scary. I don't want to be scared by God. I was scared enough in my childhood. I heard this wasn't that kind of place.

Bill: Do you want to talk about that?

Teresa: Every time you turned around someone was saying you were committing a mortal sin. Well, I just don't believe that because it made me miserable. God can't be like that. God put us on earth to enjoy ourselves and that's what I've decided to do with my life. Be nice to people. Help when I can. But have a good life.

Bill: So if God were next to you, He wouldn't scold you. He'd give you a sense of enjoyment.

Teresa: Yes. And he would understand why I've done the things I've done.

Bill: You want Him to understand you. Why don't you sit down tomorrow morning and have coffee with God?

Teresa: Coffee with God! I'm afraid. I don't know what I'd have to say to God.

Bill: Well, that was just an idea. Maybe you'd like to write a letter to God. Tell him how you think and feel.

Teresa: That sounds like fun.

Bill: You can rip it up if you don't like it. Send it or rip it up. Focus on what it is you want from your time here.

Teresa: Yes. I think I could do that.

Bill: Just begin. Tell Him you're hoping He'll understand you.

Let it flow. Don't be concerned about grammar mistakes or whether it's right or wrong.

Teresa (hesitantly): You don't want me to give it to you?

Bill: No. We'll just talk about it.

At first, Bill thinks that the generous care of the parish priest may be the entry point where Teresa can recognize God's love for her. He asks her how she feels about him, but she is unable to talk the language of relationship and reverts to her desire for a pleasant experience. Bill, then, tries to open up the possibility that she might have deeper desires. The suggestion that she have a conversation with the Lord over coffee falls flat, but she responds favorably to his suggestion that she write a letter to God.

Passage to growth

A younger person of whim generally grows through putting discipline into his life. He follows the "normal" pattern of growth from the instinctive to the moral-ethical levels that Kierkegaard describes. An older person of whim, especially one who has reverted to whim after unsuccessfully coping with the law (as is the case of Teresa), may move more quickly into personal relationship, which is the realm of faith. Usually, this person also has to put discipline into his life; but love and a sense of responsibility motivate the choice of order rather than fear or guilt.

The movement to new growth, for the person of whim, generally happens through the person's norm for life, i.e., his feelings. More often than not these feelings are negative—dissatisfaction, emptiness, a growing feeling of meaninglessness and lifelessness. The satiation with pleasure has failed to make him happy. He begins to suspect that his way of living has been unhealthy. He may begin to experience the "sting of conscience." Not infrequently, the addictions of food, drink, drugs, gambling or sex have led to such dissatisfaction, frustration, depression, or a deep fear of death that the person decides to re-examine his life and is willing to make some important decisions so that he can find life. Getting disgusted with others' remarks about his being overweight, or having a car accident while driving and being drunk, amassing large debts, getting caught in an adulterous relationship, or a spouse's decision to leave may jar the person to his senses so that he can no longer blame others for his situation. Frequently the person of whim has been so caught up in immediacy that the environment has really been dictating to him; but, with the coming of some crisis, he begins to feel that he must choose for himself. Often enough he realizes that he must change and that change must come from within and not from others.

The person of whim searches for freedom. At his core, he deeply desires freedom; he wants integration, self-knowledge, and self-possession. He wants freedom from the uncertainty in which he finds himself. But he does not know how to be free and he finds himself in a constant tension between his surface desires for spontaneity and his deeper drives for integration.

He wants to be free *from* that which binds him and he wants to be free *for* living a healthy and integrated life. Often people of whim speak of needing to get on top of their situation or to put discipline into their lives. They know that the way they have been living has been death-dealing for themselves and for others. Their choices, therefore, need to exclude certain behavior by the exercise of willpower and discipline. They need to choose life in a positive way.

The person of whim needs to begin by making small choices—experiences which produce success. Having an achievable goal or a sense of purpose can give the person of whim a sense of dignity. He begins to order his life in such a way that self-control becomes a goal rather than immediate gratification. As the search for meaning develops, his sense of priorities and values shifts. He needs constant encouragement that he is on the right path. Often a director or friend will practically have to make the choices for him—he possesses so little sense of self. Failures will inevitably happen, which can easily discourage the person of whim. He needs help to find some set form of discipline which will give him enough security to search for true freedom.

Lack of discipline in his behavior presents the biggest obstacle to his growth. He has constantly yielded to addictions—be they food, drink, sex, gambling, drugs, work, whatever. These addictive behaviors only lead him into further disillusionment. He can identify with St. Paul: "The good I want to do, I find myself not doing; the evil I want to avoid is what I do." (Rom. 7:14) With Paul, he wonders: "Who can save me?" As he wrestles within himself, he constantly hopes for a miracle. Someone else must rescue him.

Pain seems to be one way in which the Lord tries to get through to him: the pain of having no purpose, the pain of chaotic existence, the pain of dissatisfied relationships, the pain of not being able to accomplish a goal, or the pain of not being relied on by others. The dying process for the person of whim may take a long time before the person will even begin to face the question of his own unhappiness. Only after the emptiness and pain of living a life of selfishly yielding to his own feelings finally dawns on the person—frequently through some traumtic event—does the person become angry enough to begin to think about changing. Initially, he directs his anger outward—generally upon authority (God, parent, Religious Superior, or society) or a loved one. For a time he may rationalize or bargain, striving to decrease his addiction out of fear. But in no way does he want to give it up or to accept an "all or nothing" situation.

Let us pick up again the story of Teresa. It is now the fifth day of her retreat. Bill has continued to suggest to her that she write letters to God, and Teresa has responded well to these suggestions. On the third day he suggested that she have God write a letter back to her. It was a moving experience in which God told her not to worry so much and to let Him love her simply as she is. Bill suggested that, since she was beginning to find a God different than who she thought He was, she might want to write Him another letter—this time about her son Bobby. Teresa had some hesitations; but, since her other letters had proven so fruitful, she decided to go ahead with it. Now she reports on her experience.

> Teresa: You know, I really didn't want to write that letter to God about Bobby. I washed clothes. Then I washed and set my hair. Finally, I went down to the river. I took my journal along and thought maybe I could write the letter there.
>
> Bill: You were afraid to write the letter?
>
> Teresa: Yes. I just sat down by the river. The water was so clear and the sky so blue. It seemed so peaceful, so innocent. I felt like

such a contrast. (crying) I've been so selfish. I've just been running from life. My work in the parish is just an escape. I don't want to talk meaningfully with my husband. I certainly don't want to talk with him about our son Bobby. I've been angry at him because he wanted us to start practicing birth control. I've been blaming him for Bobby's birth defects. And I've been so selfish towards Bobby. I've been an awful mother because I just couldn't bear the pain. (cries again for some time) I stayed at the river a couple hours. (slowly) The river seemed so peaceful and steadying.

Bill: Somehow you drew strength and courage from the river.

Teresa (slowly): Yes. (pauses) I didn't write the letter to God yesterday about Bobby; but I think I'd like to try today. I went back to my room yesterday afternoon and started to write a letter to my husband. I just poured out my feelings. At first, I was angry; but then I realized that Bobby's birth must have been hard for him too. Maybe he's running from the pain through all the time he puts in at work. We have to talk honestly about Bobby. I know, too, that I've got to make some changes in the way I relate to Bobby. That's a little frightening, but maybe you can help me.

Bill: It sounds like a lot happened yesterday. Though many painful things surfaced, you don't seem overwhelmed by them. You seem less afraid of them and more willing to face them.

Teresa: Yes. The river was calming. I guess God spoke to me through the river.

Teresa has gradually begun to confront the reality of her life. The little successes of writing honestly to God about her life have given her strength to face her fears. She recognizes how she has escaped facing her pain through her compulsive activity in the parish. In owning her own anger at her husband, she is graced with the recognition that he, too, probably flees from his pain. She knows she has to make some choices: to talk honestly with her husband about Bobby and to let Bobby touch her heart in an affective way.

Her conversion from whim was less traumatic than many. Her experience at the river, as well as her preparation for it in the previous days of retreat, steadied her to accept the pain she had been fleeing. Most probably, she will continue along the path she has begun to move into the realm of personal faith, i.e., she will begin to grow in personal relationship with God as is described in Chapters Six through Ten. However, when most people of whim experience a conversion, they begin the more ordered way of life described in the previous chapter on the person of principle.

Summary

The person of whim is a person operating at the instinctive level described by Kierkegaard. He makes choices which foster his own pleasures and avoids pain. Ordinarily, this person grows through putting order into his life. After a life of being caught up in the immediate, he begins to realize his unhappiness. At first, he may try to increase gratification; but when this fails he will turn his anger against others or his environment (school, job, family, roommate, spouse, or community). He may toy with making some minor changes in his life, like stopping drinking for a while or terminating a relationship. But these few changes will not satisfy. Ultimately, the pain will probably increase and a certain discourgement will set in. A traumatic event may even escalate the pain. He must face the truth and make radical changes in his life. These changes will either lead to the ordered life of the person of principle or else begin the personal relationships of a life of faith.

The author's dealings with the person of whim have been mixed and limited. Usually, if a person of whim seeks the help of a spiritual director, he has already begun his conversion process. Most of the time the conversion has been at the level of religious behavior rather than at the level of religious commitment or personal relationship. The Spirit seems to call the person of whim into an ordered existence, a disciplined life, and a fidelity to self, others, and God. The Spirit calls him to set aside old habits—perhaps all at once or, usually, to change his dispositions first and then slowly to change his habits. The person begins to think about God's commandments and about what is right and wrong and then to commit himself to doing good and avoiding evil.

4

BELIEF IN GOD AS PUNISHER

More and more Americans have come to realize that they often view themselves as less than adequate as persons. Teenagers fall short of their ideals, mothers and fathers judge themselves as less than what they ought to be as parents, priests and religious have low self-esteem, and the elderly judge themselves as useless. These attitudes deny the Christian truth that each person is good and created in the image of God. Dealing with one's poor attitude toward self constitutes a crucial passage in the process of personal growth. In fact, it is *the* crucial passage for most people into the realm of faith and religious experience.

When one lives in the realm of faith, he experiences a personal relationship with God. As this relationship develops, he gains a sense of his own uniqueness and worthwhileness before the Lord and before his fellow human beings. He has passed through other stages of development: gratification of his own individualistic needs, excessive dependence on peer approval, and a blind conformity to social customs and laws. All of us pass through these stages before becoming an adult. Hidden beneath the ordinary passages—for most people— lies an innate dislike of self caused by one's inability to measure up to the idealized image of self that he has appropriated.

In the Bible God reveals that He has created us good and that He loves us as we are. Each person faces the challenge to believe this and then, as a result, to love others freely. The poor self-image blocks the achievement of these goals.

In the introduction we spoke of Kierkegaard's three levels of growth. Most frequently, a person moves from the moral-ethical level to the level of religious faith through a successful confrontation with his own dislike of self. God facilitates this process through the action of the Holy Spirit. Usually the person begins to recognize his or her own negativity towards self and God calls the person to a basic self-acceptance.

This negativity towards self surfaces in three significantly different ways: 1) a chronic and deep-seated negative judgment about self which may only be healed through therapy; 2) a growth process in movement from adolescence to adulthood; and 3) a moderate recurrence of previous negative attitudes toward self at a further stage in the process toward maturity. In this chapter we shall examine two people: Betty, a person with a chronic poor self-image who could profit from therapy and Pete, a young man in the process of claiming his identity. Many spiritual directors facilitate the process of growth which occurs in the normal passage to self-acceptance, whereas they do not ordinarily have the expertise to deal with the person who has the chronic and deep-seated negative judgment toward self. Yet it seems important to describe both situations, since both types of persons approach the spiritual director. The spiritual director also deals with the recurring instances of the poor self-image that happen in the living out of an adult faith. Most people maintain some degree of a poor self-image throughout their lives, which usually surfaces at a time when they are especially vulnerable or hurt. We shall not directly treat of this situation in the book, but the principles and procedures outlined in this and subsequent chapters are applicable.

BETTY: A PERSON WITH
A CHRONIC POOR SELF-MAGE

Betty is a forty-five-year-old woman religious who entered the convent at the age of eighteen because she could no longer endure her family life. She saw what a horrible life her mother had to live and wanted none of that. Besides, she judged religious life was a better life, since she thought it brought a person closer to God. When she first entered, she sought to please the novice mistress. Generally, she felt inadequate among her religious sisters. For the last twenty-five years she has been teaching grammar school children in primary grades. None of her work has brought satisfaction. She has always had problems living in a community of women, often feeling hurt and upset. For years she lived in depression. She became involved with a male teacher who eventually dropped her. She tried a leave of absence, but she still felt depressed; so she returned to religious life.

She has made several eight-day directed retreats and one thirty-day retreat without experiencing God's love for her personally. She has been seeing her spiritual director every four weeks over a ten-month period. What follows is an excerpt from one session with her spiritual director.

Tom: Hi, Betty. Good to see you.

Betty: Hi (smiling), I'm so glad to get together (frowning and then smiling in an apparently forced way); but I almost called and cancelled because things have been so hectic. I've just been so on the go; I've had no time. No time for anything, no time for prayer. (Pause, frowning again) Yet just this week alone I've read four novels. Community has been terrible. I just find it hard to even sit through supper. The others seem so close; I feel like an outsider. Two days ago I had an accident with my car and so I've had to borrow Sr. Monica's car. I don't like that. I worry about doing something to her car now. I'm just all messed up. Each time I come here to see you it's like a broken record: I've been running, community's been a problem, I haven't prayed. What's wrong with me?

Tom: So, you're dissatisfied with the way things have been going.

Betty: Yes, and most of all I am dissatisfied with myself. It's the same old thing. I'm just no good. This has been going on for years. This year it's Sr. Monica who keeps hurting me by what she says and doesn't say; in previous years it was somebody else. Always somebody. I get so upset and then I go off and do something impetuously. The car accident happened because I was so upset. Last week my boss asked me to think about whether I want to stay on; he's about to fire me, I guess. I feel so stupid. I'm just no good; I'm always messing things up wherever I go.

Tom: Your frustration is strong and has been persistent. You can't be the way you want to be. And you are judging yourself to be stupid, messed-up, and ultimately no good.

Betty: Exactly. And nothing seems to help. (Begins to cry. Sniffles) Since I've been in therapy, the doctor keeps helping me to see that I've not been making choices for myself. I've been waiting for God to change things or to change me. He seems so distant. Why has He let all this happen?

PETE: A PERSON GROWING THROUGH A POOR SELF-IMAGE

Pete is a twenty-five-year-old and has initiated spiritual direction in order to get close to God. During his teen-age years he stopped attending church and became "over-involved" with a girl sexually. A few years ago he experienced a conversion; somehow God touched him. He knows the Lord loves him, even if he is not always perfect.

Pete works part-time in youth ministry. He enjoys working with the kids when things go well and tenses up when things do not go well. Pete readily gets down on himself. He worries a lot about how he comes through to others. At times he gets caught up in fears, especially when he undertakes something new in his job. What follows is an excerpt from the third spiritual direction session.

Pete: Hi. I'm really glad to be getting together today. There are several things I've been wanting to talk over with you.

Sr. Joan: Well, Pete, I'm glad, too, that we are here.

Pete: Something has come up with my work. I've been so uptight lately. I don't know what's going on. I've been listening to the other people in the ministry office and figure that I really don't live up to their standards. When I'm alone with the teenagers, I'm okay if I sense they like me; usually I like them then. But I get upset with the kids who clown around. And when I get with people my own age, like to give a talk in front of them, I get sweaty and start to freeze up. I guess I keep worrying. Like the drama I had to do with Nancy. I was so afraid that I'd forget my lines that I was restless all night long during my sleep. As it turned out, I didn't forget my lines; in fact, (laughing) Nancy did—she blew one whole section. But it worked out all right.

Sr. Joan: So, at work you've been somewhat anxious, worrying how you come across, whether you measure up, especially when you compare yourself to those with whom you work.

Pete: Yes, and thoughts about the future keep coming up, I see that Nancy's become engaged and my friend, Joe, knows he will begin work with an accounting firm next fall. I don't feel ready to settle down yet. I wonder what's wrong with me. What I really want is to go south and get away from home. Yet I'm not sure that's what I ought to do. My family is here and we are pretty close. And my friends are here too. It's scary to think about picking up and moving on. Still, I've been thinking about doing just that this summer. I want to do some things I've never done yet. The problem is: I'm afraid I'll go back to my old ways and leave the Lord, fall back into the same rut I was in a few years ago. (Smiling) But I'd still like to risk it. (Pausing, looking down, then frowning) I don't know if I can do it. (Looking up) I've got some self-confidence this year. Just last week my boss stopped me to tell me how pleased he was with my work. That was good. I'm not sure what I ought to do.

Sr. Joan: It sounds like you are beginning to think seriously about your future. Moving on appeals to you. It's like you are not Nancy or Joe, like you have got to live your own life.

Pete: That's it. But it's so scary. Last month, when we talked about trusting myself and my own reactions to things—that really made a difference. I've begun to feel good about me. In the last couple weeks, there have been two relationships, you know, close ones, where I've just been myself and (smiling) that's turned out really well! I think I'm learning to trust myself.

Sr. Joan: I get the sense that you are really pleased with that approach.

Pete: Yes, it's been helpful. Occasionally I fall back into worrying about what I should do. Like the next year, although I'm not positive what the right thing is, I want to go south. If that's a mistake, I'll have to accept that and so will my family and friends and even God. They love me and I think they trust me.

Sr. Joan: So, you are willing to risk making a mistake in order to be who you are.

Pete: Yes, that's it. My dad wants me to join him in his business, but I don't think I'm ready for that yet. I do wonder why I'm not settling in the way everybody else is. But I can't knock the way my life has been going.

Sense of self

The person with a poor self-image feels hemmed in by structures and weighed down by life's circumstances. He complains of being needy and dependent. He feels guilty, for nothing he does seems right. Often feelings of inferiority erupt into anger. At times loneliness overwhelms him and leads to self-pity.

As we listen to Betty, we pick up her discouragement and her deep underlying anger at her situation, at God, and at herself. She has lived doing what she thought she was supposed to do both at home and for years in the convent. She wants to change; in fact, she chafes under the bridle of living up to others' expectations. Though her present way of living upsets her very much, she still does not know what would please her. Self-pity and self-doubt have entrapped her. She faces a brick wall no matter which way she turns. She feels guilty, for nothing she does seems right.

Often her feelings of inferiority erupt into anger, usually at her community. In years past she focused on someone else; now she focuses on Sr. Monica. In moments of greater honesty, she acknowledges that she is really angry at herself because she finds herself in a rut and keeps repeating non-life-giving patterns. She dislikes her impetuosity and the fact she keeps getting upset with others. She feels responsible for the chaos in her life and has sought therapy in the hopes of freedom. She has little sense of her own self-worth. She very much needs therapy if she is to uncover her true self. The more she owns her anger—at self, at others, and at God—the more cut off she feels. At times her loneliness overwhelms her and leads her to self-pity.

Pete's situation is different. He has escaped many of the structures which once hemmed him in. He has let go some of the external references for "good" behavior. He has not yet fully found his true "self," but he has made a beginning. He desires freedom: freedom from the bondage of those feelings which burden him and seem to impede his inner peace. In the past he put himself down and dwelt on the negative. He embraced "shoulds" which he could never reach. There was always more that he could do and a better way that he could do it. He has made a lot of progress toward trusting himself and no longer fears making a mistake. Lately, however, he finds himself again trying to measure up to others' standards.

The person with a poor self-image constantly looks to others, compares himself with them, and judges them better.

Pete's experience is not a-typical of many young adults breaking beyond that pre-adult self with its family and peer expectations and beginning to define self as unique. Most frequently, this sense of self comes through achievement in work and satisfying relationships. Pete is in the midst of claiming his own identity slowly. He has done what he wanted to do—ministry—this past year. He has succeeded in his job, although he measures his success by his feelings (not all of which have been pleasant). Though his employer appears more satisfied with Pete's performance than Pete, his own expectations for himself are beginning to fall into line with reality.

The worry and fear that Pete experiences are part of the self-growth process. At the level of behavior, Pete functions satisfactorily. His own self-confidence lags behind the objective fact; yet it continues to increase. Hopefully, Pete's own choices will bring about clearer self-appropriation and will solidify his sense of self as a unique person. As he makes choices in accord with his deeper desires, he will become more alive, more secure in himself, more free and less taunted by worry and anxiety. The choice facing him about leaving home and not joining his father's business will be a crucial step in his own passage to self-appropriation.

Sense of the world

Our initial contacts with Betty and Pete give no indication of their sense of the world. Often enough, a younger person

with a poor self-image operates with high ideals and expectations. The world does not measure up to his strong sense of
justice. But, though evil pervades, he still secretly expects that
things will change.

An older person with a poor self-image tends to be more
cynical. Often he does not see beyond himself; but, when he
does, he projects upon the world his own inner life, and
exaggerates the wrong in the world. Hopelessness pervades his
reading the morning newspaper. People hate one another.
Nations and governments cannot be trusted. He reacts with
frustration rather than compassion to the violence in the
world—a frustration that is akin to the frustration he has with
himself. The person with a poor self-image generally wallows
in a sea of blaming, bitterness and anger toward self. But rather
than accept his anger he projects it outward upon other
people.

Within our own country a strong negative self-image has
sometimes motivated both national pride ("My country: love
it or leave it") and national criticism (in the name of social
justice). The person with a poor self-image easily focuses on
what is wrong. The zealous patriot often finds the social
activist threatening the stability he needs in an otherwise
hostile environment. The zealous activist often focuses his
pent-up negative energies on the evils of an unjust society. The
frenetic activity and the ultimate hopelessness of certain
individuals in both groups indicate that something else other
than pure love is operative, namely a poor self-image.

Both the older person who has become embittered on life
and the younger person in the normal developmental process
of reaching adulthood have high ideals which do not correspond to their experience of reality. They need to know that

the world is basically good and that individuals are created unique and good by God. A person will never really see the goodness of others if he does not see the goodness of himself. For a healthy sense of the world he needs to have a balanced sense of himself.

Experience of God and prayer

The person with a poor self-image often sees God as a judge, a policeman, or a punisher. God is a taskmaster who controls the universe and "poor little me." If God wanted to, He could change my situation. Since God is all-perfect, He cannot be touched by my miserable state. God sets standards to which the person cannot measure up. The person experiences God as impersonal and withdrawn.

The person with a poor self-image feels unworthy to be in God's presence and is somewhat wary of God. He judges God untrustworthy since He permits the pain in his life. Despite his constant efforts to please Him, God never seems satisfied. God wants more and more. Since the person experiences no warmth in his relationship with God, he keeps Him at a distance.

The person with a poor self-image does not know how to pray because he does not have a sense of self which he can entrust to the Lord. He runs away from living and praying in the here and now and prefers to dwell either on the past where he remembers his failures or on the future which he fears. He spends time in prayer wrestling in his mind, debunking the positive in his experience and skipping over what might open doors to a positive experience. He constantly compares himself with what he thinks God expects of him. His prayer takes on the form of a monologue with himself which puts himself down.

We shall continue the conference with Betty.

> Betty: Nothing seems to help. (Begins to cry. Sniffles.) Since I've been in therapy, the doctor keeps helping me to see that I've not been making choices for myself. I've been waiting for God to change things or to change me. He seems so distant. Why has He let all this happen?

> Tom: So, you are frustrated with God. You know He could change things if He wanted to. And He seems so far away.

> Betty: Yes, I have been frustrated with God. I'm just a terrible person. No one should ever get angry with God. Yet it is His fault. He is so safe; He does not have to face these horrible feelings. I wish He'd make things different. (Pausing) Yet, (thinking) yet, I know I don't want Him interfering in my life. (Beginning to cry again) I don't know what I want. Last time we met I decided that my problem was that I was not putting in enough effort at prayer, so I decided to write in my journal every day after forty-five minutes of prayer on the scripture of the day. I tried to put in the time, but I was filled with distractions and daydreams and continued to worry about what the day would be like. So, after two days, I decided that it wasn't going to work to try to put time in for prayer. Prayer wasn't the answer. All I could do was think about the problems with my community, the problems at work, and I kept having all these sexual temptations.

> Tom: What did you do with them?

> Betty: For a while I got stuck in them and then I got up and moved around. In fact, I walked into our little chapel to try to get rid of the temptations and distractions. But it didn't help, so I

> just kept fighting them until the time was up. (Pausing and then looking up and in a frustrated tone of voice) What's wrong with me? Why can't I even pray? Why won't He change me?

Betty acts like a little girl who blames God for her problems. She does not know yet how to be in relationship with her thoughts and feelings; she judges that she cannot talk with God about most of her experience (problems with community, work, and sexual thoughts and feelings).

She imagines God as controlling her life. He has given her ideals to live up to. Yet He has left her alone, distanced Himself, and not protected her from messing up her life. She wants God to take responsibility for her life and make some changes in her life. She blames Him for not rescuing her. She judges that she cannot change, but that He must change her. She denies her responsibility and gives Him full responsibility. She is angry at God for letting her suffer this way. Since she cannot bear being angry with God, she turns her focus back on herself and dislikes what she sees.

Because she does not think the Lord can love her in her own experience, she has difficulty focusing on the Lord and quickly gives up her attempts to pray. Obviously, Betty has a false image of God. Let us see what happens when the director tries to help Betty see her notion of God and change it. We continue the previous conference.

> Tom: So you took efforts to get rid of what you thought was unacceptable in you, almost as if God did not want to hear about your problems and temptations. He is not the kind of God who would be interested in your concerns and feelings, especially sexual feelings.
>
> Betty: I never thought of that. (Smiling) I suppose He might be

interested. But I didn't bring that part of me to Him. I messed up again.

Tom (Avoiding her focus on herself as "messed up"): You did not think that He was interested in all of you, especially those parts of you which you find unacceptable. You have been choosing not to bring to the Lord in prayer those parts of you which seem unacceptable. Yet, you want God to change. Maybe He is inviting you to change your choice. Maybe He is distant from you because you have distanced yourself from Him by screening out much of yourself which you judge unacceptable for relationship with Him.

Betty: Why didn't I think of that? It seems so obvious. I just don't know what is wrong with me. You have been so helpful; but I'm so stupid. You are so close to God. I just wish some day I'll be there. I really appreciate your help. When am I going to learn?

Tom takes more initiative with Betty, trying to teach her that she can bring all her thoughts and feelings to the Lord for acceptance by Him. Betty, however, reverts to her favorite topic: her own worthlessness. Tom shows her her image of God, but she automatically focuses upon herself and not upon the Lord.

The person with the poor self-image, then, seems caught in a vicious circle, unable to break through the false images of God and self. It is very difficult to be faithful to prayer, since the person does not find it a life-giving experience. Betty finds whatever excuses she can to avoid praying, but feels quite guilty about it. She simply puts in time, having little sense of a personal relationship. She keeps focusing upon herself. Her customary form of prayer is meditation, which she uses to focus on her own behavior. Sometimes she looks at Jesus as a model she might imitate. She strives to take on His virtues. Of course, she always comes up short and then becomes discouraged. She cannot bring these negative feelings before the Lord since she considers them wrong. These feelings only prove her own unworthiness and inadequacy.

Pete's situation differs. A few years ago Pete experienced the Lord as a loving and faithful God who accepts him. Pete desires to trust in God's trust of him. God, he senses, will have to accept him (and in fact will accept him). Although he fears a break in the relationship, he expects the Lord to be with him as he moves away from his familiar surroundings. He now experiences God as a companion and less as a judge who is watching and waiting for him to make a mistake. Pete's own expectations of himself are slowly falling in line with reality. The more Pete lets go the expectations that he has for himself the more real his relationship with God will become.

Passage to growth

The challenge before the person with a poor self-image is to become a true self. He deeply wants to meet this challenge; he craves self-acceptance. What this means exactly he does not know as yet. But he can no longer tolerate his present situation. Very often he senses that he has been putting incredible demands upon himself—which he cannot meet— and that he has created his own feelings of inadequacy. He knows that he must let go some of the expectations he has laid on himself or allowed others to put on him.

Usually the person moves through this passage to new growth through making a specific decision which involves self-appropriation. Various movements—positive voices toward growth and negative voices toward stagnation—surface at this time. St. Ignatius refers to these as various "spirits" and stresses the importance of discerning "good and evil spirits."

The biggest "negative voice" or temptation that the person has to deal with is discouragement. He has tried so hard in the past without success that he wonders why he should try again. He fears each new avenue to be a blind alley. He considers the situation as hopeless. He may yield to self-pity and blame others for the fact he judges himself as no good. He thinks others are laughing at him as a stupid clod. He can tell you all his faults: physical unattractiveness, procrastination, etc.

He fears true self-exposure. A young person is likely to put on a false front trying to bolster up his lack of self-esteem with false accomplishments. An older or more morose person is apt to detail all his faults. Because the person with a poor self-image has little sense of self, he will try to find out what others think and do and copy their ideas and behavior. Thus he often asks: is this what I am supposed to be doing? Do you think this is okay? He fears risking failure and strives to stay within established boundaries. He judges that he does not know how: how to perform, how to relate, how to pray, etc. He may want to run from the here and now and dwell especially on the past where he remembers his failures.

The inner voices remind Betty constantly what she really believes: "I am no good, I am stupid, I am messed up." Her performance ratifies these voices; she has failed at several jobs and at many relationships. Will she ever find her true self? Will she ever come to know the love of the true God? Will she finally at some point succeed in holding down a job that satisfies her as well as her employer? She may never answer these questions in her lifetime. Her self-hate goes deep into her psyche and soul. She may struggle the rest of her days fighting her inner voices. Hopefully, her own choice of job, friends, etc., will lead her to an inner peace and a healthy sense of self. Hopefully, she can heal the wounds of her early years through therapy. Hopefully, she will meet the God of true love as she freely lives in the present moment. Hopefully, she will one day claim her own goodness as one made in the image of the God whom she seeks.

Let us look again at the experience of Pete. Earlier we related a segment of his third session with his spiritual director. Most of that session centered on his growing trust of himself as it was emerging in his ministry. He also acknowledged his desire not to settle down yet. His father's desire that Pete join him in the family business created new tensions between his desire to be loyal to his father and his desire to claim the new self that has been emerging. Let us see what happens in the next session with his director.

> Pete: I'm really glad you could meet me today. Some things have been bothering me lately.
>
> Sr. Joan: I'm happy I was free to meet with you today, Pete.
>
> Pete: Remember last time I spoke about my dad wanting me to join in his business? (Director nods in recognition.) Well, last weekend, we were alone having a beer together in the kitchen at home and dad asked me again to join him. He gave all sorts of reasons: how he needs another person and rather than hire some stranger he wants to hire me. I really got uptight: I mean, I think I love my father and I don't want to hurt him. I feel terrible. I want to do the right thing and I don't want to be selfish. Maybe

I'm just immature—you know—wanting to go south on my own. Maybe something is wrong with me that I am not settling down the way my friends are. (Nervously shaking leg) I don't want to be selfish. I want to be loving. I keep thinking that someone who has such a good father *should* help him out, should stay by him; I think that's what I should do.

Sr. Joan: So, you are thinking that a loyal son ought to show that fidelity by doing what his father wants, to please his father.

Pete: Yes, at least I wonder about that. But I keep thinking about setting out on my own, getting a job in the south, and finding out who I am and if I can handle life in another environment. I'm really attracted to doing that. That's what I desire. But I feel so selfish, so self-centered. That is what I desire and want for me. I question whether that is the loving thing to do. And I'm afraid, too. What if I go south and can't handle it? (pause) I don't know if I can leave my family; I don't know if I can survive without the friends I have here. I know I need friends, wherever I will be. And I wonder what will happen with my life in God; I mean, I don't want to get back into the drug and sex scene of six years ago. I don't think I will, but I'm scared that maybe I'm fooling myself.

Sr. Joan: The conflict is within you: some conflicting thoughts and feelings going on inside you as you prepare to make a decision.

Pete: Yes. And I have to make a decision. I've written some letters and have several job offers in the south. I don't want to let this thing just drag on; yet, (smiling) sometimes I think that I won't make a decision, but I know that deep down I will make a decision.

Sr. Joan: You do want to make a decision. But you are unsure what to trust: the "oughts" which are stirring around inside or the "desires" to move on which keep coming up.

> Pete: Yes, that's it! When I feel good about myself and think of all the good things that have happened to me these last few years, when I trust myself and the experience of God in my life, then I know I want to move on. But then I wonder how loving and how mature I would really be if I did that; is moving on selfish?

> Sr. Joan: The key seems to be whether you feel good about Pete, whether you trust God's trust of you.

> Pete (With a gleam in his eye): I have been trusting myself more and more. It has been good. I think I know what I'm going to do and I'm hoping it will work out; but I'm not sure, and that bothers me. It's a big risk.

Pete is beginning to recognize more and more the voices that lead him to life and call him to believe in himself. He is beginning to trust that God is and will be with him. He realizes that he could choose to listen to the various negative voices which clamor for attention: all the "shoulds," the downgrading of himself, the fears that he cannot make it on his own apart from his family. He can choose to resist the temptation to see those things which bring him life as being "selfish" because they do not conform to others' expectations of him. He can choose to pay attention to his feelings, to own them, and even to express them. He can choose to do the things in which he succeeds.

The choice towards life that Pete is making involves a dying process. He must let go trying to prove his worthiness. He must accept his limitations and his own goodness. Pete has already taken some steps towards the radical freedom of self-acceptance. He experienced deep freedom in his choice to go into ministry. Yet he has not yet become radically free. We saw in his third session with his spiritual director how the students challenged his self-image and how he was comparing himself with his peers.

Pete will probably choose to go south, but we do not yet know whether this will lead to a radical acceptance of self. He has the opportunity—especially if Pete experiences and believes in his father's love for him as he chooses to go contrary to his father's wishes. In the process he might feel a tremendous anger at his father and then at himself "for not living up to his potential" and "for not being a dutiful son."

Pete faces the challenge to stop trying to earn others' love by what he does and to accept the fact that he is loved simply for who he is. With this realization he can let go the ideals he has set for himself and cannot reach, ignore the negative voices that do not lead to life, trust that his successful experiences flow out of a worthwhile self, believe that those who have befriended him have done so because they have liked him and because he is worthwhile, and trust that his father loves him no matter what—even when he goes contrary to his father's wishes. In choosing "life," gradually he begins to see himself and his life with different eyes. He recognizes his own giftedness and uniqueness. At last he can say: "I am good. I am somebody. I am me."

Summary

The person with a poor self-image feels trapped and hemmed in by structures. He feels angry and generally projects that anger outward at others and perhaps God. Down deep he is angry with himself and his own inability to feel successful before life's challenges. He is tremendously disappointed in the world either because of his idealistic expectations or painful experiences. He sees God as controlling his life and feels he never measures up before Him. Thus he fears God's punishment. Negative voices continually put the person down and lead to self-rejection and self-pity. The positive voices toward life call the person to trust himself, his experience, and the good opinions of his friends.

The passage to growth is the passage to self-acceptance. It usually happens in a risk-taking choice, in which the person lets go of trying to measure up to his own and others' ideals and expectations. Very often it involves going against his fear that a given choice may be selfish. Freedom happens as he trusts that he can take the risk without fear of punishment.

5

THE SPIRITUAL DIRECTOR'S FACILITATION OF GROWTH PRIOR TO A PERSONAL RELATIONSHIP WITH GOD

To live fully as a Christian one must accept himself and believe in the Lord's unique individual love for him. The previous chapters have described the ordinary passage to growth by which people begin to claim themselves. In describing the persons of principle and of whim, as well as the person with a poor self-image, we have attempted to delineate persons who have reached the levels of development that Kierkegaard calls the moral-ethical level and the instinctive level. Such persons have not claimed their identity or entered into a personal relationship with God.

Generally, the process of claiming self involves facing one's own poor self-image. At times the person so rejects and hates himself, as exemplified with Betty, that referral to psychological services is appropriate. No matter how much Tom tried to lead Betty to focus on the Lord's love for her, she continually reverted to her own worthlessness. She kept the focus on herself rather than on God as she refused to let love in.

However, whether a poor self-image weighs the person down or not, whether a person needs professional counselling or not, God still calls the person into relationship with Him. A spiritual director can facilitate a real relationship between the person and himself and can be very helpful in facilitating a real relationship between the person and the Lord. This chapter describes the spiritual director's role in this process.

The persons described in the previous chapters do not relate in a personal way with others; they do not know who they are and who the other is and thus cannot enter into a personal relationship. Their world centers on themselves, especially their own feelings and ideals. They need a sense of reality. The director provides an objective sounding board, especially for the persons of whim and those with a poor self-image who need to know their own goodness and cease running from the truth of that goodness. Reality does confront them. When the director reflects back to the directee what reality is saying and how others are responding to him, the person receives a new perspective and is no longer caught in his own subjective feelings. Sr. Joan does this very successfully with Pete. He easily recognizes the truth of what she says and is eager to respond and grow. He is in the normal process of growth. Tom has much greater difficulty in getting Betty to act upon the objectivity of his feedback. Her negative self-image is just too all-consuming. Bill helps Teresa get a greater sense of objectivity by having her own her feelings in writing letters; but the real breakthrough in objectivity for her comes through nature, through the peace and security she feels at the river.

The objective response has less effect on the person of principle who generally has an idealized self-image. No objective response that his pastor can give about his homilies is really suitable enough. Phil understands his pastor as presenting an ideal to him, in the same way that he preaches down to the people. The person living a life of principle needs feedback on his or her own subjectivity and interiority. The person of principle focuses on ideas and ideals. Freedom and growth lie in becoming aware of one's feelings. The person of principle is caught in generalizations. He needs to become aware of his own specificity and uniqueness, generally through recognizing the uniqueness of his feelings. The person of principle has been controlling his feelings, since he is afraid of risking loss of control. The director expresses interest in each feeling and experience. Very often the person has developed certain stereotypes from his culture which block out the reality of his own experience, e.g., the person may judge that it is "wrong" for a man to feel tenderness, or for a religious to have sexual attractions, or for anyone to feel sad. He may even have created certain masks to hide the way he feels or even *that* he has feelings. The director desires that the person of principle will have the courage to be himself and will surrender all the masks which have been used to cover up both gifts and weaknesses. With encouragement, the person of principle will begin to live in the acceptance and enjoyment of his feelings. He is not discovering his feelings but rather his self in a way that surprises and delights even as it may confuse. The person begins to claim his self as special and unique. What before he knew intellectually as good he now experiences as good.

Phil begins to get in touch with his own subjectivity after falling in love with Ginny. The older priest encourages him to own his feelings and to bring them before the Lord in his prayer. His own compassion for Phil allows him to listen lovingly and quietly to Phil's struggle. He calls Phil to acknowledge his inability to control his feelings and to bring his powerlessness to the Lord. Basically he challenges Phil to let the Lord love and accept him in his own uniqueness and subjectivity.

All of these people (Teresa, Phil, Betty, and Pete) speak in generalities and need to be encouraged to be specific, especially in self-disclosure. Often the person with the poor self-image speaks abstractly and puts himself down with vague generalities or vague comparisons of himself with others. In helping the person be specific, the director will encourage the person to look back on individual past experiences and to claim the good that has been there. He will help him to talk about his feelings as "my feelings of" and to begin to know his own inner life in detail. Sr. Joan has much greater success in helping Pete do this than Tom does with Betty because Pete has achieved greater freedom. Bill accomplishes this small goal with Teresa through suggesting that she write letters.

The director encourages these people to focus on the positive by searching out the good in their lives and noting the places where they have felt alive. The director encourages them to move with that life. He can help the person focus on those experiences where he felt blessed or called to life: times of joy and creativity, times of awe and wonder, times of loving and being loved. Further, the director can encourage the person to continue to trust that God really wants him to be happy rather than "perfect" and miserable. He fosters the person's making choices which bring success and enjoyment. The director helps the person realize that God wants him to be full of life and to savor the joy of being alive. Sr. Joan has a great deal of success in helping Pete do this and, eventually, the older priest has some success with Phil. The person of whim also needs encouragement, real goals he can reach, and praise for his accomplishments. Discipline, sports, job, family, and education all provide opportunities where this might happen. The director can also help him notice the positive responses that he has received from others and help him to trust those responses. The person of whim needs some dignity and pride in himself. Bill guided Teresa slowly in making suggestions to her that she felt she could carry out.

The director may suggest that the person who has not claimed identity be kind to himself both in thought and in action. Issues such as fun, relaxation, wasting time, and conversations with others, can open the doorway to a life of affective experience which precedes deeper religious experience. The director must instill in the person the realization that taking time for himself and respecting his own desires are healthy and not selfish and that he need not fear pride at his own success. The director should attend to images that occur in the directee's consciousness, especially images of life. A tree, a river, a bird, an insect, frequently something in nature will speak life to the person with a poor self-image. The director encourages the person to unravel the image.

The director helps the individual to discern spirits through focusing on the positive. He unmasks the destructive voices that do not bring life. He points out what the person really dislikes and yet chooses; he points out attitudes within the person which continue to weigh him down: the comparisons with others, the high ideals he has for himself, and the tendency to focus on what is wrong. The director brings light to the directee. Bill speaks candidly of Teresa's fears and encourages her to explore them. The directors of Phil, Betty, and Pete show them their denial of experience and feelings.

The director also encourages changes in non-life-giving attitudes. The person of principle knows well the negative in life and in himself. Though he needs to accept his weaknesses, and though the director's acceptance of his weakness is helpful, it is more important that the director help him focus on the positive. The person of principle has usually been so busy trying to win others' love and approval that he has generally neglected the gift-dimension of life. He does not really believe that God loves him uniquely and wants to gift him with his deepest desires. Phil exemplifies this struggle for acceptance.

Every process of growth is difficult, but we cannot underestimate just how difficult it is to accept oneself and one's being loved. The person of whim fears that putting order into his life may destroy his very self. The person of principle fears losing control if he begins to face his feelings. Fulfilling the law has given him a certain amount of necessary but limited security. Since he is afraid to risk, the director should support appropriate risks that the person might take to overcome the limits of living on principle alone. He encourages him to trust himself and his ongoing experiences. He reminds the person that the Lord has been faithful in the past and will not abandon him in the future.

A key area of risk is that of relationship. Entering a real relationship often provides the cutting edge for the person's growth. Phil's growth most dramatically depicts this situation. He discovers both his attraction for and his fear of intimate relationships. The older priest encourages him to reveal his own interiority (his innermost thoughts and feelings) and to face his awkwardness and embarassment at revealing himself.

Frequently, in his self-disclosure, the person of principle tends to generalize and speak abstractly. A good director patiently encourages the person to be specific in his self-disclosure. The person of principle, especially, has not honestly and openly entered into interpersonal relationships with others or with the Lord. He has not accepted and trusted his feelings and experiences. The director's own relationship with him provides an example of how to build relationships. His openness and freedom model self-disclosure and facilitate the directee's articulation of self-understanding.

The person's openness and trust of a director often precedes his openness and trust of the Lord. The director keeps pointing the person to the Lord. However, the directee may be reluctant to open himself before the Lord—even if he is actively religious and has been praying for a long time. Thus the director often teaches in the beginning. He encourages the directee to expand his image of God and the scope of God's love, as well as to expand his understanding of prayer. Many things can be prayer: walking in the woods, choosing life, choosing not to follow negative impulses. The person will experience tension letting go his images of God as Judge or Punisher and accepting the Lord's love and mercy. He learns that God even accepts his failure to let go his false images of God. So, slowly the person experiences the full acceptance of the Lord: nothing need block the Lord's love for him. God wants only that this person be himself and not some idealized image of who he thinks he should be. The real person begins to emerge and finds that living prayer means living the person that he discovers himself to be. The person stops trying to earn love and opens himself up to accept God's love and acceptance. Writing "letters to God" and "letters from God" can facilitate a concrete, honest, and dynamic relationship with Him. The spiritual director encourages the person to be *human* in prayer, as well as in relationships. He suggests that the directee bring all his feelings—those judged positive and those judged negative—into relationship with the Lord. Claiming one's feelings (be they tenderness, delight, sexual attractions, or sadness) helps the person grow in trust of the Lord's acceptance. The backlog of thought and feelings which have prevented his claiming his own unique self hinder his openness with God. He thinks it is selfish to accept his own individuality. God cannot love him in such a way that he receives what he really wants. God loves one who sacrifices, not one who gives into whims. Over and over again priests and religious have struggled dramatically in choosing to alter their own vowed commitments. In this choice for self, they feared being selfish and offensive to God. What a tremendous pain for the person who has been consciously striving to be good and to please God! The director stands with the person in the pain and calls him to face it with the Lord.

Gradually the person recognizes those impulses which lead to greater negativity and those which lead to greater freedom. As he begins to distinguish these impulses, the director helps him associate God with the latter movement and a non-God force with the former. The director helps the person focus upon the Lord and not upon himself, especially looking beyond those things about himself which he dislikes. Here the director's role shifts from teacher to guide. He leads the person to a knowledge and experience of the true God. As the directee grows in self-knowledge, he begins to realize and to believe that when God made him, He created him good.

The director encourages the person to listen to the Lord and

to His words: "I forget the past and am doing something new
... You are precious in my sight; I love you." (Isaiah 43)
"The love I speak to you about is not your love for God but
God's love for you first ..." (1 John 4) God becomes one
who loves unconditionally. He soothes the soul. The person
learns that God is with him, for him, and even within him. He
desires more eagerly that presence. The director invites the
person to take God's love inside himself and to savor it. The
person begins to trust this new God as someone who lavishes
good things on His beloved.

As the relationship develops, the guide becomes more of a
spiritual director. He asks more and more: "Did you bring that
to the Lord? What did He say?" The director needs to be
gentle, but firm. He sends the person to the Lord, suggesting
that he speak his mind, heart, thoughts, and feelings to the
Lord and that he wait for some response. He invites him to a
real relationship. He encourages him to talk to the Father and
to Jesus as friend to friend. He waits patiently as the directee
takes two steps forward and one step back.

The director takes very seriously God's present encounter
with the person in the concrete "now" moment. He keeps
challenging the person to be real and , in doing so, to realize his
goodness and lovableness. The person with an idealized or
with a poor self-image realizes his goodness when he stops
trying to earn love and opens himself to accept God's love as it
comes to him in his own unique experiences. The Lord calls
him to accept himself as good and as unique. The director calls
the person to receive God's acceptance. The director gently
guides the person to look at and to listen to the Lord's total
love. He invites the person to bask in the embrace of the Lord.

Part II
Faith in a Personal God

6

BELIEF IN GOD AS CREATOR

A person moves toward claiming identity when he makes the leap of faith in his own value as a person. He recognizes himself as a good person, loved and worthy of love as he is. This experience constitutes the "Principle and Foundation" upon which his whole growth in the spiritual life rests. If a person does not believe in God's genuine deep unique love for him or her, he cannot claim self. Instead, the person's Christianity, Catholicism, or religious life focuses on his external behavior. Directors of the *Spiritual Exercises* have encouraged the retreatants to spend several days contemplating their own unique experience of God's love for the purpose of securing and deepening this foundation. Thus a journey begins that will last a lifetime: a focus on the Lord's munificence in loving first and foremost.

At this stage of development a person grows through abandoning himself to the Lord, really revelling in the goodness of self, others, and God. Later the person will discover evil in himself and the world and God's attitude toward evil, but first he must revel in goodness. He must embrace the uniqueness of himself and others and exult in this, just as God does. He must trust his own goodness and use his gifts, talents, and person for others. He must believe in their goodness and call others to believe in it as well. He must let go of the cynicism that would put a distance between others and him.

He must let that life that is God's come alive within himself and vivify him. Nothing escapes the Lord. A person can use any experience for God's glory and the building of His Kingdom. Generosity, eagerness, and trust well up within the person as he rejoices in the goodness of all creatures. Thus as his gratitude increases, he yields more to the power of being which is already at work in the world and within himself.

There follows a conference between a director and Mark who six months ago fell in love and is planning to get married in about a year. He is twenty-seven years old and has been receiving spiritual direction for about two years. He sought spiritual direction originally because he wondered about a priestly vocation. In the process he discovered his own dislike for himself, dealt with it, and has grown in self-acceptance.

> Mark: Things are really going well. Sue and I are spending a lot of time together. We looked for furniture last night for the apartment. (Beaming) The wedding Mass and reception are pretty well lined up. We're even getting the parents to go along with some of the things in the liturgy. In fact, (teasingly) they might even be ready to have you do the homily. What do you think of that?
>
> Sr. Barbara (Laughs): Well, things are really going well. All you'll have to do now is to convince the priest! (Both laugh).
>
> Mark: Things really have been going well. Last Saturday Sue and I went on a picnic together. It was a warm sunny day. We saw squirrels and rabbits. We even played kickball with some little kids. A lot of laughs. And on Sunday we went to the zoo.

We took Sue's little brother Stevie—and he was a perfect angel! I couldn't believe it! But he enjoyed the monkeys and the seals. And we did, too. And things have been going well with her father. I guess he's really not that bad. I decided to get my hair cut and the night before last we bought me a new pair of slacks. (Winking) But I'll still wear my jeans at home! I have been praying, and all these events have been part of my prayer. I just really feel grateful to the Lord for all the good He's letting me experience. This is the happiest I've ever been!

Sense of self

Mark's fundamental outlook has to do with goodness. The world is good; God is good; he is good. He knows he is loved for who he is and he can claim his own goodness and love. Everything about him speaks of life and he delights in the events of his life. He rejoices in the goodness of others—even the pesky Stevie and his prospective conservative father-in-law. He exults in life and wants to live it to the full. He feels valued as someone and thus can be playful.

This stage of a person's development corresponds to the "identity" stage of Erikson's theory with some beginnings of intimacy. The person senses his or her own goodness and feels worthwhile. He experiences a joyous, relaxed, playful atmosphere. He wonders at the beauty of life and of creation around him, at the beauty of other people and even of himself. It is great to be alive! The new discoveries about himself excite him. He thirsts and hopes for growth. Gratitude pulses through his being—gratitude for all life—and he eagerly desires to experience it all. He exults in just being himself. He knows himself as gift—created out of the goodness of God and mirroring that goodness.

Mark knows he has a place in the world, with something to do and to contribute. He has a sense of ordered priorities, of certain values being more important than others; yet he also possesses a freedom and a spontaneity. The desires to please and to do the right thing no longer dominate him; or rather, when these desires surface, they pale before his positive experience of God's love incarnated.

Mark has a deep sense of being gifted. He can do. He can be. He can sing; he can praise; he can give thanks; he can yield and let go. He can achieve and succeed. He can make decisions. He has an initial sense of his freedom. Though tentative, he desires to open his hands to the Lord as much as possible, not yet knowing what that means. He has already experienced himself as letting go a bit, is amazed at this, and feels very grateful. He hopes it will continue.

Mark manifests a peace and radiance. He walks firmly with a confidence in himself. He is buoyant and light and possesses a good sense of humor and good eye contact. The person who experiences himself as loved feels comfortable with himself and with others. He feels at ease with his body. He sits erect, yet manifests an obvious freedom of movement. He smiles easily. He manifests a care for his person in his groomed appearance.

Sense of the world

When a person experiences himself as loved, he sees the world most positively. His optimism extends to all levels of creation: inanimate matter, humanity, and the universe as a whole. He sees the goodness of inanimate creation in a new way as if for the first time. He admires and gets caught up into the mystery of it all. He awakens to God hidden in "many dappled things." The balance of the seasons, of the cycles of life, and of the reproductive systems in nature all speak the joy of living. This focus pulls him outside himself, beyond self-preoccupation. As the person gets caught up into the mystery of evolution, he often desires to maintain the precious wealth that the earth offers us. Thus he may become concerned for the environment, with anti-pollution laws, energy conservation, and maintaining the gifts of nature.

Such a person also has a deep sense of the beauty of all that is human. Cherishing the fact that each person is a child of God and a unique participation in His image, he appreciates the multiplicity and pluriformity of all peoples. The variety of races, nations, customs, cultures, and languages all manifest the vitality of God. He desires that every person develop his capacities and find fulfillment. In this context he desires the equality of opportunities for all and freedom from deprivation and dependence. Thus, at this stage of development, he can champion human rights; but, ordinarily, he will not have much understanding of the complexity and the evil involved. Very often such a person gets involved in peace movements.

Possessing a simple optimism and a winning generosity, the person is generally a joy to be with in his youthful enthusiasm. He finds life meaningful and God everywhere. He dwells in the positive qualities of humankind, seeing all of us as brothers and sisters. Frequently, he is blind to the obstacles to fulfillment, growth, and freedom, not yet knowing the realism of sin and evil. The person may concretize this stage of development by becoming a zealous missionary whom others may see as a "do-gooder." This sort of optimism pervaded much of the era of the 60's in the United States.

Experience of God and prayer

If the person claiming identity is accustomed to religious language,[1] he sees himself as filled with an awareness of God. God seems all-pervasive. He has been with the person through his past, gently holding him and prodding him. Now he surrounds the person and dwells within him. He beckons him toward the future. He challenges him to grow. God is good and to be trusted. God is love; God is life.

The person speaks easily of the goodness of the Lord and His fidelity throughout his life. God radiates life and loves him uniquely. The person relishes beauty—the beauty of nature, the goodness of people, the joy of life. He speaks of his thirst and hunger for more; he is eager to search , to risk, to explore.

He imagines God as a person who, like the Hound of Heaven, has relentlessly pursued him with love. God has lovingly created and fathered him. He has been concerned for the person throughout his life, even though at the time he was probably not aware of it. The person now accepts God's love interiorly. With a deep sense of providence, he imagines God as powerful, generous, magnanimous—most good, kind, and understanding. God personally invests Himself in his life.

Praise and gratitude characterize this person's prayer. He focuses on the goodness of self, others, the world, and God.

---

[1]The movement of the Holy Spirit will manifest itself if the person says "yes" to the invitation. One can say "yes" without naming it in the traditional language of God. Belief, trust, and charity increase in the one who says "yes." The quality of life changes with each affirmation, surrender, and embrace.

How great it is to be alive. His experiences speak of God's providence and personal love. Let us pick up again Mark's conference with Sr. Barbara as he begins to speak about his prayer.

> Mark: . . . I have been praying.
>
> Sr. Barbara: So even your prayer life has been really good.
>
> Mark: Most of my prayer has been praise and thanksgiving and I've used a lot of the Psalms—Psalm 138, 146, 103. Also some of the songs from Godspell have been going through my head—especially the song "All Good Gifts." I really want to praise Him. One day last week I had the image from Isaiah 49. (fighting back a tendency to tears) I was being held in the Father's hand, lovingly and gently. (slight pause) I keep noticing how neat nature is: the picnic and the zoo. I know God is there. It's just great. Even my friends. They're just good people. Even Stevie and Sue's father. In fact, people have been wonderful to us since we announced our engagement. (Quietly) And I know God's given me all that. So you can see that God's been so good to me, and I'm just so grateful to Him for the things that are happening to me and for the people in my life—and most especially for Sue. Last night after we had shopped, Sue and I came back and lit a candle. I put my head on her lap and we just prayed together. We composed our own Psalm 135. We took turns naming each blessing the Lord has given us and we said together after each "for Your great love is without end." It was something special. And then we were just quiet for a long time watching the flame of the candle. It was a holy moment. . . .

Mark's prayer shows his familiarity with God and his sense of God's pervasiveness in his life. There is nothing pretentious about it. God's love is just there—a gift to be relished. When he feels especially moved by God's care, he wants to cry, and he is almost moved to tears without embarrassment as he recounts this to Sr. Barbara. He knows Sr. Barbara understands and will rejoice with him in God's kindness to him.

Passage to growth

As the person initially claims his identity he may have a difficult time articulating his desires. Since he enjoys life so much, he wonders if he is escaping reality. Life cannot be this good, but, no matter what happens, he continues to feel himself blessed. He articulates his desire as a desire to be open to whatever God wants. We saw this in the previous dialogue between Mark and Sr. Barbara. Mark desires to embrace life in all its forms and to grow in self-knowledge. He wants to spend his energies for the Lord and serve others. He wants to continue to be loved and to love and to enjoy the process. He simply wants to be with God, to savor that presence, and to be grateful for that reality.

Though the person at this stage of growth may not be able to voice it, he wants, at this deepest level, to enter fully into the experience of God. He wants to savor life and himself and to relish the goodness of all creation. He moves through this passage by accepting himself as being loved.

Certain voices foster this growth and call him to enter deeply into the flow of life and to affirm his own goodness, the goodness of others, and the goodness of God. The good spirit calls him into the mystery, wonder, and surprise of life. The Spirit leads him to thirst for more. It will call him to claim himself and to use his talents; it will call him to risk and to create. Now is a time to choose happiness, joy, beauty, and truth and to concentrate on their presence in the world. The Spirit will lead him to take risks, to plunge into life, to let go, to choose the more even if somewhat timidly.

Other voices try to cut short the joy that he is experiencing and lead him to a premature and false "death." The evil spirit points out his imperfections and unworthiness to be loved. His evil—evil itself—is too big for God. How can God love him? He may fear he is fleeing reality and that his joy cannot be soundly based. The evil spirit strives to undermine the healthy self-confidence and joy that the person has been experiencing. It may lead him to doubt God's love and his own goodness. It strives to make him doubt the goodness of others and to be cynical about the positive affirmation and support they may give him. Ultimately the evil spirit, especially through fear, strives to undermine the sense of self and of God's unique love for him that he has only so recently acquired. Before this sense of God's love has been firmly established, the evil spirit may lead him to focus on his own sinfulness and unworthiness, a proof that God could not love him.

We pick up again with Mark four months after his marriage. We see the subtle voices that have begun to undermine his sense of God's unique love for him and his sense of his own goodness and worth.

> Mark: I really needed to get together with you tonight. Work's been going okay, and Sue's fine—in fact, she's perfect. But I am really down on myself. Two Sundays ago we were having dinner at her folks' place and I had this big argument with my father-in-law. I don't think he respects me, and since then I find it hard to live with myself.

Sr. Barbara: Are you respecting yourself? (Mark puts his head low and sits quietly for a while.)

Mark: I know I'm just not measuring up as a husband or as a son-in-law. Sue's so cheery in the morning and I can't say anything until I've had two cups of coffee. What's wrong with me? My father-in-law's a bigoted conservative who just likes to pick a fight. And I don't want to fight with him. I'm just a coward. I don't have the courage of my convictions. And, on top of this, I can't pray. God just seems distant.

Sr. Barbara: You really are seeing the negative side of things again.

Mark: Yes, I guess this is pretty negative, isn't it? It's more like our conferences of two years ago.

Sr. Barbara: What did you learn two years ago?

Mark: I learned how I can tend to exaggerate the negative—especially in terms of people's responses to me. I project on them feelings that they don't even have. I make myself responsible for their behavior. And ultimately I judge myself as inadequate alongside of them.

Sr. Barbara (with teasing tone): Well, I'm glad you learned all that two years ago and have never had to battle with those negative voices again. (Mark laughs.)

Mark (smilingly): "I've really been on a bad trip over myself, haven't I? I know Sue loves me whether I'm chipper or not. And I know her father just likes to argue. It doesn't mean anything else. And I know God loves me no matter what. He's hit me over the head with that so often—gently.

The person beginning to claim identity experiences a

movement deep within him toward something new. He desires to be filled with life, to be loved, and to be more free. But to fulfill his desires he must let go old securities and die to his own efforts at self-perfection. Often he has to die to the categories he had of God or the limitations he put on God. God becomes all-permeating love or all-penetrating life, pulsating through the reality of all creation, personal experience, and inner being.

At first, however, the person tries to ignore the call of love and life to him. The call may surface when he is attracted toward another person or when he first hears about a positive experience—the directed retreat or Marriage Encounter or a charismatic prayer group. Some initial invitation or prompting happens which the person chooses to avoid. In some instances, he may even become physically ill (a sign of hidden conflict) as he chooses avoidance, since deep within him he wants something more.

As the good stands before him and beckons him, sometimes the person grows angry that his plans are being messed up. Generally, however, it is fear rather than anger that surfaces. Thus every messenger of God's love or Good News says, "Do not be afraid." The person fears God's coming close. In terms of personal development, he fears anyone coming close because they will see his unworthiness. Even if the person has already experienced his own goodness, as in the case of Mark, he still experiences helplessness and fear before the gratuity of such love and life. He feels his own inadequacy before this goodness. He is being asked to surrender to the gratuity of being loved, a way of living that shoves him out of control into receiving the gift.

We pick up Mark several months later.

Mark: I'm not sure what's happening. Sue has been so good to me, so accepting. I'm grouchy in the morning and tired when I come home from work, yet she never complains. I want to pay her back and show her how much I love her, yet that doesn't seem to be what God is asking of me. He keeps telling me to let Sue love me. I'm afraid. I don't know what this means. I mean (pausing)—I want Sue to love me, but I also want to show my love for her. But I don't seem to be able to. I fear I'm going to become a nobody. It just doesn't seem right. I keep thinking about my father and how he loved my mother. He seemed so attuned to her needs and he would do little things to make her happy. It's like nothing I do—or even what I don't do!—makes any difference. Sue still loves me. (Pause) I'm afraid. I don't like it.

Sr. Barbara: So you appreciate Sue's love for you; but you're also in touch with a fear. Her love seems too good and generous. You'd rather earn it or prove yourself worthy of it.

Mark: Yes, I'm uncomfortable with it being so freely given.

Sr. Barbara: It's like maybe it's saying something about you or about relationship, and you're afraid of what might emerge.

Mark: Yes. I'm afraid of being so passive. I fear I'll be a nobody. And I guess I also fear that it won't continue. If I don't deserve her love, then she may stop, and I'll be very hurt and crushed.

Mark experiences tension within himself. On the one hand, he is drawn to this full passivity of letting love in and even feels called to this by the Lord; yet he is also afraid. He wants to earn Sue's love lest he not be a self, lest he be an empty nobody. He fears the future: how can Sue continue to love him if he passively accepts her love?

Some people will fight and bargain and perhaps allow

themselves to experience this gift momentarily—like on a retreat or in certain circumstances or with certain people—but not radically. Some never let love and life inside them. They refuse to surrender to being loved because of fear that they may be overwhelmed or lose their identity or be hurt.

Sometimes the person needs to heal some memories before he can surrender. Frequently one needs to examine some relationship, e.g., with his mother or father, before he can surrender to the challenging and unconditional love of God who is Father and Mother. Many people do not successfully pass through Erikson's stages of trust and autonomy in their early years and deal with the hurts of these years in the process of claiming their spiritual identity.

A person achieves spiritual identity through surrendering to being loved unconditionally. In the process he lets go his trying to control his own destiny. He experiences a radical act of trust and owns a healthy dependence in being loved. He surrenders unto Another as he is because the Other loves and initiates that love. Small wonder that Ignatius saw indifference and all spiritual growth flowing from this.

The second passage through which a person passes in his spiritual growth is the passage through which he allows himself to be loved. Through this passage, he fulfulls his desire to claim his own identity. Having moved through the passage, a person is able to revel in his own goodness, the goodness of creation, and the goodness of other people. At the deepest level of one's being a person needs and wants to be loved for who he is. Though this means that he wants to be loved in his weakness and sinfulness, that is, totally, it seems that he needs first to be appreciated and loved in his goodness.

A perduring poor self-image or feelings of inadequacy and

guilt can block a person's acceptance of God's love throughout his life. So, too, can the clinging to past security. Generally, a person subtly desires to earn love rather than simply accept it. He fears that, unless he earns it, he will not be lovable. He also fears he may not have a self at all, if the self that he has is only gift. The tension between having a role to play (one's creating himself) and grace (the gift of self from God) is as old as the human race. God's love summons the person to yield to His power and let go into love.

7

BELIEF IN GOD AS SAVIOR

The awareness of oneself as good, as a person uniquely loved by God, is a tremendous grace. The ancient Hebrews articulated this in the very first chapter of the Old Testament: "And God created man and woman . . . and God saw that it was good."

The grace of the earlier movement, however, while being a tremendous and liberating grace, is only part of the grace of self-acceptance. One's being stretches beyond his goodness. He is also a sinner. At his deepest core he is a loved sinner.[1]

For the purpose of analysis, it seems helpful to divide the reception of this grace into three stages: 1) the initial stage; 2) the struggle; and 3) the acceptance. We shall use the situation of Sr. Shirley, a Vicar for Religious in a large diocese, as she meets with her spiritual director, a young priest named Mike.

---

[1] In his *Spiritual Exercises* St. Ignatius speaks of this grace as the grace of the first Week.

A. THE INITIAL CALL TO DARKNESS

Shirley has already wrestled with her desire to conform, her perfectionism, and her own poor self-image. Though she enters those spaces from time to time, she has tasted a deep freedom and joy in the fact that she is loved by God and by her fellow men and women. She has tasted beauty and given herself to it. In all these experiences she has felt joyful, exalted, and innocent. She has experienced her life as a pure gift. In other words, she has experienced the grace of being loved in her goodness.

When a person has experienced himself as loved and worthwhile for some time, his previous joy and fervor either gradually or sometimes suddenly disappear. The person experiences shock and confusion. Where before all was light, now the person finds himself in the dark. Life is gray, heavy, and empty. Below is an excerpt from a conference of Sr. Shirley where she begins to discuss this change with her spiritual director.

> Shirley: I've been trying to pray the passages where I've experienced the joy of the Lord's love for me. But they don't work any more. In fact, I have no taste for prayer. I feel like a dry well. I've been putting in a half-hour at prayer, but nothing seems to help.
>
> Mike: It's been a hard time for you.
>
> Shirley: Yes. It's like the brightness of the light has dimmed and twilight and darkness have settled in upon me. I wonder what I'm doing wrong. I've done some examining of myself, but I haven't come up with anything. I'm afraid. I know how down on myself I once was and how unbelieving I was in the Lord's love. I don't want that to happen again.

Mike: So you have done some self-examination and come up with nothing.

Shirley: Yes. I don't understand what's happening. I felt so sure of the Lord's love before and of the many blessings He's given me. But now everything seems so empty. Frankly, I don't like what's going on. (Pause. Nervously wringing her hands and looking out the window.) I don't know. Maybe I don't know myself as well as I thought I did. What do you think I should do?

Mike (ignoring the last question): So once you felt so sure of the Lord's love for you and your own goodness, but now things seem so empty and dark. You feel confused about what's going on and even unsure about yourself.

Shirley: Yes. I noticed I'm more on edge in my work and in my community. I've been staying away from people for fear that they'll find out what I'm going through.

Mike: It's pretty hard to be in the state you're in.

Shirley: Yes. I really don't like it. I can't even read the newspaper in peace. I mean, I try to believe in a good God who loves His people, but all I focus on in the paper are the killings and the fires and the wars. I want to ask how a good God can let this happen. But I know something is wrong with me. So I keep asking God to give me different lenses with which to view what's going on in the world.

Mike: So it's even hard to look at what's going on in the world.

Shirley: Yes. God seems to be withdrawing from the world and He's also withdrawing from me. I don't know how to respond to Him. In fact, I can't even find Him. I feel so lonely. I don't know what's wrong with me. What do you think I should do?

Mike (again ignoring the last question): God seems to be withdrawing from you. Have you asked Him why?

Shirley: Well, yes—or maybe no. I guess I just figured it was my fault.

Mike: Maybe you want to ask Him again about this.

Shirley (hesitantly): Yes, I think I should. (Pause) And I want to. I really don't like what's happening; yet, I also want to get to the bottom of this. I'm afraid and I want to run; yet, I also have the feeling the Lord wants me to listen to this experience. Does this seem right? I want to be faithful; I want to do what He wants. There's been no relief or peace in the running. I want to trust Him.

Mike: So, though you don't like it, you have a sense that you're called to remain in the darkness and explore it as the place where God might be speaking to you.

Shirley (hesitantly): Yes. I guess that's it.

Sense of Self

The darkness surprises Shirley and she does not understand it. She yearns for her past consolation of the Lord's presence. In her head, she believes that God still loves her and she wants to trust her belief. But she cannot help asking: "*Why* has the Lord gone? What have I done wrong?" These questions riddle her being. Though she wants to look honestly at herself, she fears falling back into her former self-hatred. She also suspects that there are many hidden parts of herself. Her efforts to convince herself that she is okay or that God will soon return seem empty the longer she remains in the dark. The feeling of loneliness and isolation only intensifies her self-doubt. Though she fears her empty feelings, she also senses herself on the edge of mystery which is drawing her. Though she wants to escape the dark, she has an inner sense that she is to remain and even to explore the dark.

The person being drawn into darkness often appears restless. Hands fidget; the face can appear bored, the eyes distant. The person's spirit seems listless; if he smiles, it is a forced smile. He chatters rather than speaks substantively; he may even complain or whine. Initially, he tries to deny the experience, with the expectation that life will return to the joyful innocence of being a loved creature. He tries what has "worked" in the past and wonders if that will work again. His memories recall the "good old days"—his first personally directed retreat and various Scripture passages that have been meaningful in the past. He becomes more and more confused the longer he remains in the darkness and tries various remedies. If the person has been somewhat irregular in spiritual direciton, he may now begin to see a spiritual director again in earnest in the hope that the director may know what to do. He may want the spiritual director to rescue him from the pain and darkness. He may want to be parented and to have the director make his decisions for him, as we see Sr. Shirley do a couple times in the conference. He may try to play on the sympathies of the director or close friends, though more than likely the person fears disclosing the darkness to friends.

Since she has deeply experienced the Lord's love in the past and wants to trust the Lord in spite of her doubts, she wonders if she should trust the Lord in this experience of darkness.

Mystery seems to call her to explore the darkness. In the Rules for Discernment, St. Ignatius tells the spiritual director that there are three reasons why the Lord might have a person experience darkness: 1) to give him a new revelation of his own sinfulness; 2) to purify him from his desire for consolation, and 3) to let him experience the depth of his creaturehood and his utter dependence on God.[2] Often all three are involved and the spiritual director watches them unfold even without the person's awareness of them.

Sense of the world

In the beginning stages of recognizing the world as full of sin and one's own complicity in sin, the person is unable to admit his sin. Sin looms clearly before the person, pervading the television and the newspapers. But , as with Sr. Shirley, the person cannot accept fully the reality of it, since sin seems to deny the goodness of God. Thus Shirley prays for other lenses with which to view the situation. Usually, this type of denial does not govern the person too long simply because of the reality of evil abounding.

Experience of God and prayer

There is a gradual transition in the person's image of God as he moves through the dying process of becoming loved as a sinner. When he enters the experience of darkness, he

[2]*Spiritual Exercises*, 322.

struggles for an image of God. Before he imagined God as a powerful creator; now, though he still believes in God's power and presence in his life, God seems distant and almost silent.

Prayer is dry and difficult. The person is confused as to what is happening. If he remains faithful to prayer and does not give up because of lack of "results," he hungers for his past feelings of consolation. He may try harder for a time, but eventually the person usually becomes discouraged. His prayer may become "whiny" and complaining. The person needs to bring his confusion to the Lord and trust that He is at work.

Passage to growth

The most important choice that the person makes at this point in his or her growth is the choice to keep focused on the Lord and His love. Specifically, he chooses *not* to focus on self, but rather to enter the darkness in a spirit of surrender to a loving God. This trust in a loving God manifests itself in being faithful to prayer, in not making any specific changes in one's schedule, in resisting escape and avoidance (for example, sleep), and waiting patiently for clarity.

The person finds himself with ambivalent desires. Thus, on the surface, Shirley's fear is strong, and she desires to get out of this darkness, to go back to her former joy, to change this present situation. She wants to get out of this entrapment of self at any cost. But at a deeper level of herself she wants what the Lord wants. She wants to be real and authentic. She wants to surrender deeply to the Lord; and, if this darkness will lead to that, she wants it.

Because she navigates in uncharted waters, she is most vulnerable to different voices. The positive voices call her to accept the reality of the past and present and to enter the experience of darkness. In the initial stages of experiencing the call to be loved by God as a sinner, the positive voices call the person to remember God's love for him in the past. They call him to accept God's goodness and fidelity, even though he does not feel them at the moment. They will challenge him to trust this present sobriety as good and even to enter the darkness, trusting in the fidelity of the Lord.

The negative voices at this time in a person's development take the form of doubt and discouragement. They tempt the person not to believe his past experiences of God's love, but to consider them as sham and delusion. They tempt him to return to those Scripture passages that once brought him life and to dwell on past favors of the Lord's love, not to buoy him up for his present struggle, but to regain a lost paradise and to flee from the present call. They taunt him with the fear that the Lord could not love him in his darkness. In the extreme case, rather than run from the dark, he may seek to plunge himself into a consideration of personal sin in a masochistic attempt to relieve the guilt and doubt he feels in the dark.

B. THE STRUGGLE TO LET GO

Perhaps the clearest way to describe the person as he moves more deeply into the recognition of his own sinfulness is to follow the stages that Elizabeth Kubler-Ross has outlined in her analysis of the process of death and dying. These stages are a fruitful avenue for understanding many of the experiences of growth in faith in one's life. She describes five stages: denial,

anger, bargaining, depression, and acceptance. In the preliminary movement of being drawn into accepting God's love
for him as sinner, it is denial that is largely operative though
the person may experience some anger and bargaining. The
denial generally takes the form of the person's belief that all is
okay and that he will return to his former state of happiness.
The person denies his call to a new stage of growth. The other
stages will involve both a progression and an overlapping.

We shall continue to use the situation of Shirley. Ever since
she began to feel restless, she has been seeing her spiritual
director every two weeks. Of late she has been feeling down.
This has been going on for five months. There follows an
excerpt from their conference.

> Shirley: Well, I don't know why we're getting together today. I
> have nothing new to say. There's still nothing spiritually going
> on. It's just very dry. I keep waiting for the Lord to do
> something. He just doesn't act.
>
> Mike: So your prayer continues to be dry. We talked about your
> dryness a lot the last time we got together.
>
> Shirley: Yes, and it's gotten darker. I'm beginning to feel numb
> in the darkness.
>
> Mike: Uh-huh.
>
> Shirley: It's like I'm paralyzed or as if I'm mired in a swamp and
> I'm sinking. I'm reaching out trying to grab on to something. I've
> fasted from desserts. Everything my community does just
> makes me angry. They're late for meals. No one helps with the
> cleaning or dishes. Nobody else will take Vangie (Sr. Evangelista)
> to the doctor's. Ugh! (Breathes heavily) Oh, I know I'm just
> being critical. Something's wrong with me. I'm trying not to
> burden others with my anger or my being so down. I've been

looking for ways to pick me up, but none of them seem to work. I try to smile, but I'm afraid they can see that it is all so false.

Mike: So you've been doing everything you can to get out of the swamp and you can't.

Shirley: Yes, and I'm frustrated. I don't know what God wants. (Starts to cry) I feel like I'm innocent, that I don't deserve this! I've tried to be good. It's true I may not be perfect, but I still feel I don't deserve this. God is all-powerful. He could take this away. He would take this pain away if He really cared. How can a good God do this to me? How can a good God allow me to suffer this way? I'm not so certain He really did love me in the past. And not only me! I can't bear to read the newspaper or watch the news on TV. We are so inhuman and so unjust to one another. We can't get ouselves out of this mess anymore. Only God can do it, and He doesn't even care! Sometimes I get so mad at Him. I've pounded my fists on my bed, but He doesn't do a damn thing! I've fasted, but what good does it do? I've tried to get others in the community interested, but they don't care. They've just given up. What's the use? (Pause) I wish God would do something.

Mike: So you are frustrated and you're waiting for God to do something.

Shirley: I wish He would hurry up.

Mike: Maybe it might be helpful if you tried to pray some of the images that you have been given—either the paralysis or the being mired in the swamp. How does that sound to you?

Shirley: Yeah. I'm not sure if anything will help. I'll try. We'll see what happens.

Sense of self

After the person has been in darkness for some time, the sense of helplessness begins to overtake him. This helplessness expresses itself in anger. Often the person becomes angry at the human condition. At a given point, the person usually becomes angry at his spiritual director. Why does not the director tell him what to do? Why does the director keep telling him to stay with the darkness and bring his feelings to the Lord? He is tired of doing that. Nothing is happening.

The person nit-picks all the little faults of his closest friends. We see the way Shirley overreacts to the neglect of the household chores. Eventually, the person turns the anger on God who he judges could help him if He really loved him.

The person spends this time blaming and fault-finding, focusing the problem on others. In his anger he may shout, cry, rebel or throw things. He may seek to escape in food or sleep. His face and neck are often taut. A woman generally expresses her anger in the privacy of her room. When she sees her spiritual director, she is more apt to speak of "frustration" than of "anger."

Gradually the person vents his anger to no avail. He remains in darkness, but now begins to sense that he is at fault, that he has sinned, that he has offended God. He senses that he has committed evil and is horrified at his own sinfulness. He feels guilty, ashamed, overwhelmed by his own sin. He gets anxious and begins to panic, desiring to deliver himself from his sin.

We see the dawning of a sense of sinfulness in Sr. Shirley's previous conference. Her anger at her sisters and at God have been the doorway through which she begins to sense that something is wrong with her and that she is guilty. Thus she tries to fast. She also tries to overlook her sisters' faults. Through all these actions she subtly tries to escape the darkness and to "earn her salvation."

Some people will go to confession or tell some secret sin to another. Others may try to right some relationship where they sense they have wronged someone. Some will ask forgiveness of another or offer forgiveness to someone. Many will renew their efforts at fidelity to prayer or decide to go to church more frequently. With each attempt, the person becomes more anxious. Despite all his efforts and all his pleading with the Lord, he still finds himself trapped in darkness. At last, he has to admit that he cannot escape the darkness.

There is a certain frenzy about one's actions as he seeks to find one remedy after another and to escape the darkness without success. Though he now realizes his sinfulness, he still finds himself irritable and defensive in his relationship with others.

Finally, the person feels totally overwhelmed by his sinfulness. He feels trapped, caught, blocked, totally unworthy, separated, and alienated. He wants to give up. He senses himself a source of evil. He realizes that, despite all his efforts, he cannot remedy the situation, he cannot save himself. St. Paul spoke of this situation in Romans 7.

Thus he has become quite heavy and weighted, silent and sullen. He has lost hope in his own efforts. He feels mired in his sin and unworthiness. He tends more to withdraw from relationships and to turn his back on his closest friends. Not even they could love him in his present condition.

Sr. Shirley has not yet progressed this far in the dying process. She is still bargaining and tryng to pull herself out of the swamp through her own efforts. But we can see the beginning of the movement to the later stage of Kubler-Ross's dying process, i.e., to depression, in her speaking of being paralyzed and mired in the swamp. It will be a while, however, before she finally accepts her total powerlessness and need for someone else to save her.

Sense of the world

The person's sense of the world follows the same pattern of the dying process. In the initial stages, we saw Shirley trying to cover over evil with the idea of God's goodness. But as she loses her sense of the goodness of herself and of the presence of God, the reality of evil impinges more and more upon her experience. God no longer seems quite so good. In fact, she begins to get angry with Him as she faces her own helplessness to do much about the evil in the world. Bargaining takes the form of fasting for and with the hungry in the world; but her penance gives her little satisfaction.

At this point in her faith development she still keeps sin and evil outside herself. She feels helpless in the face of their overwhelming power. Her attempts to placate God get nowhere. She has not seen the awful truth of her own responsibility for the evil in the world. For the moment, evil remains outside her. Others are responsible, not she. Ultimately, God is responsible; He *could* take the evil away.

Experience of God and prayer

The person's image of God gradually changes as he moves through the dying process of becoming loved as a sinner. From the awareness of God as distant, powerful, and separate from the person comes the sense that, although God is somewhat aloof, He still involves Himself in the person's life. For some reason He chooses to be passive and veiled. As this realization begins to dawn on the person more and more, he gets angry that God should do this. He judges God as responsible and questions His care for him. Such an image of God contradicts the person's sense of a loving God and eventually becomes unsatisfying. So at this time the image of God becomes somewhat confused. God is still all-powerful, but the person no longer sees God's power as kindness and goodness. Rather his power is stern and demanding. He watches one's behavior. He is the Convictor, the Truth-Bearer, the Judge, the Revealer. He is Other than the person. As the sense of darkness and powerlessness deepens, God becomes a God of the dark and of the depths.

As Shirley experiences the evil in the world, she knows that evil offends God and that people have created the evil. This realization confuses her. If God is all-powerful and all-loving, why does He allow evil and sin to happen? She feels she does all she can to remedy the evil, but nothing changes. Again, her lack of success confuses her. So, at this time of development in faith, God appears as an impersonal force who controls the world and one's life while remaining aloof. He could remedy the situation of evil and sin if He wanted to; but, for some reason, He does not choose to do so.

Insofar as the person gets any sense of a personal God, God is the one offended and pained by sin. He is the Father as the Prodigal Son sees him from afar. He is Jesus who looks on Peter after his denial. But the person does not yet know God as forgiving Father or Jesus as Savior. The person has moments of being in relationship with God, but these get cut short as the person changes his focus from "God is offended" to "I offended God" to "I must make up for this offense."

The person's prayer at this time is struggling and grasping. In the anger and bargaining periods, he begs, pleads, and demands. He continually cries out "why?" and receives no answer. He cries out for forgiveness, but has no sense yet of what forgiveness means. He does not enjoy prayer; he does not like to find himself so out of control or unable to achieve. He is tempted not to pray. He looks on prayer with distaste and aversion.

In the depression stage of the dying process, he turns his anger upon himself. He moves alternately between self-clobbering and self-pity. Finally, he gives up the vehemence of the struggle and with stark faith gazes on the cross.

Passage to growth

The person is most active throughout this struggle to let go. After an initial attempt to blame others and God for the present situation, the person accepts his own responsibility. He deeply desires to remedy the situation. He is truly shocked and repentant for his sin, and he expects that, if he "remedies" the situation, the darkness and pain will leave him. Thus he may go to confession or do some penance. He genuinely wants to do "what is right" and to get rid of his sin. He also wants to get out of the darkness and he assumes that "doing right" will lead him to freedom. During this process, then, he wants to be the one in control, he wants to make up for his sins, he wants to save himself.

He desires very much to know his own sinfulness and to explore and own it. He wants to appropriate his whole self and to respond wholeheartedly. To do this he is willing to face and enter into his negative experiences. The positive voices encourage him to enter into the struggle, the pain, and the darkness. They encourage him to be real and to express his negative feelings. They move him to trust and to hope that God still loves him in the darkness. They encourage him to wait on the revelation of the Lord and to keep his focus on God who is love and on Christ who hangs on the cross.

The voices which do not lead to growth tempt him to stop the process because he fears the struggle will annihilate him. They will try to keep him from being open with the director. They will tempt him with the idea that his sin is so great, that it is unforgivable, that God could not possibly accept him, and that he is doomed. They will tempt him to discouragement.

The person chooses life through being patient and continuing to wait upon the Lord. He chooses to be faithful to prayer even when it is dry or painful. He chooses openness with God and with his director. He chooses to focus on Jesus rather than to wallow around in self-pity.

C. THE GRACE OF BEING A LOVED SINNER

The person generally remains quite some time with the sense of paralysis. Eventually, he stops fighting it and stops trying to earn his salvation. He senses that God is at work in the darkness, that it is okay to be in the darkness, and that he needs to wait on God.

Below is a conference which occurred six months later. Sr. Shirley has often been using the image of being mired in a swamp which Fr. Mike had encouraged her to use in her prayer.

Shirley: I prayed with the image of the swamp almost every day for the last month. I've begun to see some of my deeper faults. I've realized that I don't want to be weak or helpless. I've realized that I want things my way and not God's way. I realize that I don't like other people to see me as less than perfect. In fact, I think I've been denying that I'm a sinful person at all.

Mike just nods receptively.

Shirley: This has even spilled over into my sense of evil in the world. I had been blaming God and others so long. But now I sense that, as much as I hate the evil in the world, I'm contributing to it. I'm only beginning to see this. Part of it is simply the pride I've had in the human race and our ability to conquer anything. It's subtle. I need to listen more. I've remembered how many other times I've been in the swamp and I've crawled out on my own. And I realize how proud I am at what I've done. But this time I'm stuck and we're all stuck. I can't crawl out on my own. And we can't crawl out on our own.

Mike: So you have discovered you're helpless and that you've never wanted to be helpless. Now you see how proud and self-sufficient you have been. And this is also true of the human race. It sounds like you're learning a lot about the truth of who you are and who we are. It sounds like the Lord is giving you a grace, that He's revealing to you your sinfulness and just how deep-rooted sin is in the human race.

Shirley: Yes. I sense that, although this month has been very painful, it has been very good. I'm learning more who I really am. It's strange that this kind of darkness hasn't been the kind of bummer that I've had before. I haven't been down on myself. It's just been dark and frustrating, but I think God is revealing something about me and about Him in the darkness. He's also saying something about darkness in the world.

Mike: You sense you are called to stay in the darkness and that God is going to speak to you there.

Shirley: Yes. That sounds right. I don't like the swamp, but that's where I am and that's where He is, too.

We pick up Shirley and Mike three sessions later. Shirley has been getting more and more in touch with her own sinfulness, especially her core sin of pride. From time to time she has continued to use the image of being mired in the swamp for her prayer. She has owned her powerlessness and been waiting on the Lord. This waiting has been different from the restlessness and frustrated waiting that she had when she first initiated the bi-weekly meeting with Mike. This waiting has been more quiet and expectant.

Shirley (shaking her head back and forth): I've begun to see just how deeply pride has affected my life. I've never seen this before. And I've just felt powerless to do anything about it. I know now what a tremendous grace this has been. The other day at prayer I finally felt myself going under in the swamp, but no sooner was my head under than I felt someone under with me—picking me up. I was so surprised. (Slowly) At the moment that I drowned I was rescued. I had the sense of the Lord embracing me in my pride and somehow transforming that. It was too good to be true! But it *is* true! It was unearned, undeserved; I never even thought He'd do it. I was powerless to save myself, but He did it. I felt so loved, so freed, and so completely dependent on His power and His love. I am loved as I am. I am a loved *sinner*! I don't have to be other than I am. I just need to let the Lord love me.

Mike: That's tremendous! Now you know what St. Paul meant by the unearned gift of salvation.

Shirley: Yes. And it'll never be any different. He'll always be in the swamp with me, saving me moment by moment. And, although I don't understand it yet, I sense this is true of all of us, of injustice in the world. We need a Savior. God has to pick us up. I know we say that's what Jesus did in the Incarnation. But somehow I sense that has to be true today too.

Sense of self

Darkness has become the place for revelation. Shirley gradually realized her deep-seated sinfulness and became at peace with that revelation. Eventually, that revelation led to the further revelation of the mystery of God as Savior. She sees the whole experience as an incredible surprise and gift to her. The Lord often chooses to use the very image, in this case the swamp, that He uses for the revelation of sinfulness to reveal also His forgiveness.

With the experience of being saved, Shirley experiences herself as freed, relieved, and reborn. She feels alive and cherished. She is totally amazed at the bountiful love of the Lord. She knows she has done nothing to earn the Lord's love and experiences herself as gifted undeservedly. She senses she will never be the same again. Initially, she feels an incredible sense of joy and exaltation. Her ideal self has finally been broken through. She feels incredibly grateful and senses a deeper union with the Lord.

However the grace of being loved as a sinner comes, the person experiences it as totally gratuitous. St. Ignatius suggests that the person experiencing this grace place himself before Jesus on the cross. In the emptiness and dryness of depression, in the dry gazing upon the crucified, at last comes the words, "I love you. Your sin does not matter." The person is truly and deeply sorry for the situation, regretful of his own sinfulness, and the Lord says: "I know. I love you."

Sense of the world

As Shirley deepens her awareness of her own paralysis in the face of sin and then her own guilt in contributing to evil in the world, she gradually becomes aware that we are all sinners. This sense of social sin, however, dawns much more slowly than the sense of personal sin. Shirley only possesses some inklings of her own responsibility.

The more she sees injustice and social sin the more overwhelming they seem. The person feels that injustice is so pervasive and so built into the structure of our human interaction that he sees no way out. He realizes he participates in an evil much greater than himself. Only gradually he begins to see that his little compromises contribute to the conditions of poverty, oppression, and sin. Shirley is just beginning to suspect her own guilt. The realization of social sin often lags behind that of personal sin, but the process is quite similar. The more one listens to the evil in the world, the more one's sense of helplessness increases. Evil is just too pervasive. Despite one's good efforts and intentions, nothing changes. As one recognizes his powerlessness, the person begins to pray in a new way. He experiences his own paralysis and being mired in the sinful structures of our world and pleads for a Savior.

But before whatever salvation the Lord has in store for him and His people comes, the Lord will reveal to Him his own participation in the sinful social structures and how his lifestyle and his choices are permeated with sin. Thus one's sin takes on social dimensions and Christ's saving power is experienced corporately and socially.

Experience of God and prayer

As a person begins to accept his paralysis and inability to save himself, he imagines God as all-powerful and somehow at work in the darkness. God is Lord of the Dark and Revealer— revealing something very important. The person feels a sense of awe and expectancy at this time. However, he has no expectation that the final revelation will be: "I love you even where you think you are unlovable."

The person prays passively and resignedly, begging to be healed, touched, and saved. He experiences hope only when he gazes upon the Lord. He can only open his hands and trust. He knows his sinfulness, but he feels powerless to do anything about it. When he can pray, he asks to come before the Lord in his sinfulness and powerlessness. He knows he is one with all mankind. He knows he needs a Savior; yet he has no sense of what experientially that might mean.

Once the person receives the fullness of the grace, his prayer moves to a quiet gratitude for God's mercy. He desires to dwell in the Lord's forgiveness and mercy. He may experience an attraction to service as a loving response to God's love, but this attraction is silenced by his awareness of his sinfulness.

Numerous other images of God occur at this time. He is a loving Father who has always been faithful and embraces and accepts the prodigal son as he returns. He is tender, gentle, and understanding. He is merciful and forgiving, as Jesus forgave Peter on the Lake of Tiberias. He is the giver of all gifts. He is the giver of all life. He is all-holy, all-penetrating. He is Redeemer. He is the light that shone upon the person's darkness. He has enlightened his creatureliness and sinfulness; He has loved him totally. He is unchanging love. He is the Hound of Heaven. He is a God who attracts and draws the person to Himself.

Passage to growth

In the depth of the darkness and emptiness, after the anger and anxiety have finally subsided, the person feels purged and powerless. He still deeply desires to be freed, but he peacefully resigns himself to waiting upon the Lord. He wants healing and forgiveness; but he is powerless to *do* anything or to be anything other than one who waits in emptiness.

The positive voices at this time call him to trust and wait on the Lord for His healing and forgiveness. He chooses life by accepting the darkness as the place of revelation. He also chooses to let the forgiveness come and to accept being loved as a sinner. A person may also choose to go to confession, not out of a desire to cleanse himself or to be freed from the darkness but as a joyful and amazing celebration of the Lord's love.

The negative voices at this time will try to deepen discouragement and call the person to wallow in self-pity. One chooses death in choosing self-pity.

After the moment of healing and freedom, the person desires to remain there, to depend on the Lord, to rest in His mercy, and to experience further His love and forgiveness. He is filled with a sober gratitude and praise. The positive voices call him to savor the forgiveness and to be thankful for the Lord's mercy. The person experiences gratitude for having been sustained and loved and forgiven in his sinfulness. He feels awe, wonder, and surprise at his situation and dwells in quiet praise and joy. The key choice at this time, then, is to dwell in the forgiveness and mercy before rushing into activity. Often this will express itself as the desire to know the Lord more.

The negative voices at this time may call the person to deny the darkness or to conclude that, now that it is over, he will never be called into the darkness again. Most commonly, these voices also strive to cut short the deepening realization of the Lord's mercy by calling the person to plunge into activity.

Summary

We have, then, the gradual movement which happens in receiving the grace of experiencing oneself as a loved sinner. It is the fullness of the gift of self-acceptance where the person realizes that he is loved fully—in his goodness as well as in his weakness and sinfulness. The entrance into darkness as a place for God's revelation marks a crucial step in one's growth in faith. One cannot advance further without first entering this darkness. It corresponds, I believe, to the experience of the Purgative Way that the classical spiritual writers have written about.

The death-and-dying process described by Elizabeth Kubler-Ross helps pinpoint the various moments in which the grace is being given. Initially, the person struggles with accepting the reality of the darkness that has begun to enter his life. Once he can no longer deny his experience, he strongly directs his efforts toward recovering his past peace and happiness. He will blame others and God, thus protecting himself from owning his own sinfulness and guilt. When this fails to recover his past peace and joy, he will try different behaviors in an attempt to bargain with God and "earn" his freedom. Bargaining also fails. Finally, his anger at self and the feeling of powerlessness so overwhelm him that he stops trying and admits at his deepest level his need for a Savior. In His time God responds and says "I love you." Though the person may experience his sin as taken away, i.e., that he will no longer have to deal with it, more often than not he experiences being loved right in his sinfulness, i.e., he knows he is this type of sinner at his core and will remain so in the future and yet the Lord still loves him and will continue to do so. He experiences God's forgiveness as sheer gift.

8

THE SPIRITUAL DIRECTOR'S FACILITATION OF A PERSONAL RELATIONSHIP WITH GOD

The process of self-acceptance involves two dimensions: the acceptance of one's goodness and giftedness and the acceptance of one's weakness and sinfulness. Most people gradually acquire a sense of self-acceptance. Before the person can face looking at his own weakness and sinfulness, he needs first to root himself in his own goodness.

Thus the first stage of coming to identity consists in dwelling on the positive, steadying oneself in the goodness of life, self, others, and God. Though this can seem unreal and pollyannish because one tends to ignore the negative, this step is crucial. Without this positive sense of self and the world, the individual lacks the strength to integrate the negative into his life in such a way as not to succumb to the self-rejection of the poor self-image.

Thus the director encourages the person to dwell on the positive and to resist looking at the negative. He may suggest that the person look back on his own personal salvation history and re-experience the touches of God in his life. He encourages the person to rest in the beauty of nature or music, to contemplate the richness and variety of the world. He fosters wonder and gratitude in whatever way he can. He encourages the person to express his feelings, to enter deeply into relationships, to recognize and rejoice in the goodness of self and others. He encourages him to see all reality as flowing from a loving Father and pulsating with the life of the Spirit. The person prays the Psalms which speak of the goodness of God and of our gratitude in response.

Mark portrays a person at this stage of growth. His prayer naturally gravitates towards the Psalms and towards praise of God. Sr. Barbara simply encourages this. When Sue's goodness and his own sense of his inadequacies begin to undermine his hard-won positive self-image, Sr. Barbara reminds him of his earlier bouts with a poor self-image. Her teasing acceptance of him facilitates his own recognition of his present temptation.

The director's own acceptance of and belief in the person facilitate the person's recognizing that the Lord does love him and that He loves him uniquely. The director encourages the person to define himself in the face of all the loving and life-giving experiences he has had in his life. He encourages him to deeply believe and to trust the words and actions of those who have loved him. This belief grounds the person's leap of faith. Though the directee is fundamentally unsure of his own goodness, he trusts the belief of others (parents, relatives, friends, spiritual director) in him. He realizes that he has not earned their love and yet they do love him. In spite of the temptation to judge himself negatively, he has to own the positive experiences of his life and that others have responded to him favorably. Sr. Barbara skillfully helps Mark realize the gratuitous love he has received as well as the fears he has in accepting this love.

The director desires that the person deepen self-confidence and trust in the Lord so that the person can resist temptations to discouragement and self-rejection when he looks at his own sinfulness. For the person will continue to soak in and take in all of life and love until, desiring more, twilight comes. As the person focuses on and relishes his experiences of being loved, he will eventually become afraid of that love. It is crucial at this time that the director continue to point the person to the Lord rather than to look at self apart from the Lord. The person, of course, *will* look at self apart from the Lord. He will experience confusion at the change in himself. He has been basking in the Lord's love; now he senses himself withdrawing. He has gradually taken the love he receives for granted and now he becomes aware of his own infidelity.

As the person begins to move into darkness, the director wants him to remain open to the experience and to trust that it is the same loving God that he has experienced before that calls him into the darkness now. He wants the person not to succumb to his fear but to remain faithful to the process. He urges the person to go before the Lord: what does the Lord say to you in all this? How does He feel toward you?

The director needs a firm, non-vacillating approach in the face of whatever escape the person tries. Though caring and gentle, he firmly helps the person identify his denial and flight. He may explain some preliminary rules of discernment and give a clear explanation of the ways of disposing oneself to God and to the process of growth.

Shirley is surprised at the emptiness and darkness she feels. Self-examination reveals nothing. When she asks Mike what she should do about it, he ignores her question and gets her to clarify more for herself her feelings and experience. He asks her to go again before the Lord and elicits from her the fact that somehow she senses God's presence in this experience.

Shirley is being led to experience her sinfulness. After a person has dwelt a sufficiently long time on his own goodness and the goodness of God, the Lord begins to reveal to him his own negativity. The revelation comes as a shock and the person does not like it. He gets angry and tries to cut short the process. The director encourages the person to speak his anger to God and to examine his feelings of alienation before the Lord. He wants the person to be honest with the Lord. He encourages him to hope and to search for God. He encourages the person to hang in there and not to give in to the desire to avoid or to escape—even through excessive penance. He desires that the person truly feel his own brokenness. He hopes the person remains patient with himself, with God, and with others, trusting that the Lord is at work.

He desires that the person become present before the Lord, that the person bring all his feelings, desires, thoughts, and judgments before Him. To a large extent, the person will find himself expressing negative feelings and will enter spaces he will not want to be in. He will experience himself as being out of control. This loss of control is important because, until he experiences himself as out of control, he will not experience his need for a Savior.

The director may also choose to help the individual understand his present experience of desolation. St. Ignatius offers three reasons why desolation, i.e., the felt absence of God's love, occurs: 1) the individual may have done something wrong and God is attempting to bring the person to a true perspective of his behavior; 2) the Lord is purifying the individual of his desire for consolation and teaching the individual that He is Lord both in good times and in bad; and 3) the Lord is gracing the individual with an experience of his creaturehood and his inability to manipulate God or to control his life's circumstances. Often all three reasons function in desolation. The person experiences some freedom as he comes to realize that he is not the sole person involved, that life is relationship (with God), and that God's love remains active in His life even when he does not experience it.

The primary task of the director at this time is to encourage the person to keep his eyes focused on the Lord, especially Jesus on the cross. He will keep reminding him to be real and to bring his experience to the Lord. He will encourage fidelity to prayer and a wise use of penance. Thus he stresses movement toward God rather than away from Him.

The darkness may last a long time. Before the moment of acceptance, the director wants the person to yield to God's mercy, to enter and to believe in the darkness, to give up controlling his life, and to accept Jesus as Savior. He achieves this goal largely by having the person focus on the incredible love Jesus has shown him on the cross. He may also encourage the process of healing of memories.

Shirley remained a long time in the darkness. Mike simply encouraged her to remain there. Since she had been given the image of feeling paralyzed and mired in a swamp, he encouraged her to dwell in that image before the Lord. Through that image she eventually received the grace of God's gratuitous love for her as a sinner.

Once the person has said "yes" to God's mercy, the director suggests that the person savor God's mercy and deepen his gratitude for God's love before rushing into activity. The rushing into activity could become another subtle way of trying to earn God's love. The director calls the person to rest in the goodness of the Lord and the unique love He has for him.

The transformation in the person runs deep. He usually also experiences a conversion in his understanding. Confronted by the reality of God's love as he savors God's mercy and compassion, the person comes to see that only one reality matters, namely the love of God as manifested in Jesus Christ. As he basks in the compassion of the Father and the forgiveness of his own sin and sinfulness, he comes to know that nothing can separate him from love. The more a person penetrates the mystery of this love the freer he becomes to respond in love and to build God's kingdom.

9

BELIEF IN JESUS

As the Lord brings forth growth in the person who has had a profound experience of being loved as a sinner, the person experiences a beckoning, an irresistible attraction, a surge of new life. He is attracted to a person, a people, a work, a way of life. Though he personally feels quite poor, he wants to respond to the love received. The attraction to relationship is strong, like a current in a river. Often it is like a hidden current: deep but not that well recognized by the traveler.

The attraction to relationship involves growing levels of intimacy both with the Lord and with His people. Initially, he is attracted toward one or two significant others, and, later, to a more global generative loving. The grace could be termed as that of being a loved and loving disciple.

This chapter explores the dynamic of growth in faith as a loving disciple. The person comes to believe in the fullness of God as revealed in Jesus. The person experiences an overriding force to love, to be in union with another. The person will experience the dynamics of love with a freshness, will face the difficulties of loving, will learn different kinds of love (a true love and a false and deceptive love), and finally will transcend the pain of loving. Openness, risk, and transparency characterize a person's life during this era of spiritual growth and human development.

A few preliminary remarks might be helpful concerning relationship. The quality of relationship of which we speak involves intimacy, self-disclosure, feelings of attraction and delight, and the risks of communication. All of the spiritual and human growth that has happened heretofore forms the foundation for relationship. The person needs to recognize himself as both good and sinful; otherwise he lacks an honest sense of unique selfhood. Without an honest self-awareness, relationship will be characterized by defensiveness and a basic lack of open trust.

The capacity to love means that in some way one reverences and respects the other as other. He affirms the other. He desires to do for the other and to be with the other. Initially, the attraction summons forth a trust and a transparency in the relationship, as well as the awareness of one's vulnerability in being open. As the relationship deepens, so too does the vulnerability and the cost of the relationship. If one loves, he cannot escape being hurt. He is called to remain faithful to the relationship in spite of the pain, though he is tempted to cut off the relationship. He has to be true to himself and to his loving in the face of all the obstacles: self-doubt, physical nausea and repugnance, hurt, humiliation, rejection, sin, helplessness, etc. Eventually, if one grows, he accepts the pain and a quiet peace and joy perdure. The relationship may remain fragile, but the storm has been passed through. The person has been purified; he possesses an inner freedom, which enables him to let go his own needs, and an inner sensitivity, which allows him to hear and respond to the needs of the other.[1]

Thus, throughout the process, this movement toward closeness with the other leads to new risks which become growth points. One learns to listen more sensitively both with his heart and with his head. He learns to share himself much more concretely and risk deepening levels of vulnerability. Love grows to the point of transcending the faults, weaknesses, and even the sinfulness of the one who is loved. Frequently, a mutuality occurs. Feelings of joy and peace and satisfaction often accompany such growth in loving, but so do feelings of sadness, confusion, frustration, and vulnerability. There are times when one is misunderstood or when one misunderstands. Expectations and projections block the truth of the other; so these blocks must be exposed and let go of. Love wants to care for and to protect; yet so often one is not cared for or protected reciprocally. Vulnerability and pain increase only because one loves. The end of the love is union and the doorway to that deep union (relationship) so often involves the gift of loving and the pain of vulnerability. Stages of excitement give way to stages of disillusionment and discouragement, which, in turn, give way to stages of deeper closeness and a stronger union. (Books have been written on this process. It is recalled here only to point out that spiritual growth includes and involves human growth.)

Growth in discipleship normally begins with commitment

---

[1]The process described here corresponds to the dynamic which St. Ignatius outlines in the Second, Third, and Fourth Weeks of his *Spiritual Exercises*. The process involves growing identification with Christ in His mission as he responds lovingly to the Father and to His people. The person commits himself to love in spite of the cost, which results in his own "death" and subsequent glorification.

to a few significant people. This corresponds to Erikson's sixth stage (intimacy) and to the process of growth in relationship with Jesus that St. Ignatius strives to facilitate in the Second Week of the *Spiritual Exercises*. With time and experience, the process of growth in discipleship moves to a more global or general scale, to a societal love. This process corresponds to Erikson's seventh stage (generativity) and to the process of identification with Jesus in His Paschal Mystery, which St. Ignatius facilitates in his Third and Fourth Weeks of the *Spiritual Exercises*.

A. THE CALL TO RELATIONSHIP (BELIEF IN JESUS AS HUMAN)

We shall use the situation of Janet, a thirty-four-year-old religious woman who senses a call to a ministry among the poor. The initial exchange takes place in the interview in which she applies for a program which will develop neighborhood facilitators who can commit themselves to the people in the neighborhood and then, out of that relationship, help build a Christian community. A layman, Tomás, conducts the interview.

> Janet: I'm amazed that I'm here. When Father asked that I consider applying to this program, I couldn't believe it. I'm very much afraid. I wonder if I really belong here. This is for special people and I'm just ordinary. And yet, (blushing) I think I do belong here. (laughing) How's that for a combination?

> Tomás (laughing): Well, our aim is to train Christians to be servants of change, to enable others to be catalysts so that something at the structural level happens. I guess we all

experience some fear at the prospect of something so large; overwhelmed and yet drawn.

Janet: I'm not sure I understand what that means, but I do know the Lord has given me so very much and that without His power I won't be able to do anything in this program. In fact, speaking of enablement, I'll fail unless He enables me. On the one hand, this program excites me and makes me feel eager; on the other hand, I feel little and very humbled.

Tomás: Well, could we look to your strengths and weaknesses as you would assess youself for this kind of ministry?

Janet: This *is* embarrassing. I wrote them out, but it's not like an application for the many teaching positions I've held where so many of the qualifications and limits are merely external. This application seems to touch also upon what is interior. And there I felt very poor and yet desirous of giving who I am so that others can have life. (pausing) I am efficient and responsible; but negatively sometimes I can be too responsible, you know, too controlling. That's an area I feel I need to learn a lot about in this program. I'm a hard worker and generous with my time. I also know how to relax and can have fun with all sorts of people. I think there'll be a lot of that in the neighborhood. And as I look ahead I see this program as teaching me a lot about people, about myself, and about the Lord's way. I've been through a lot in my thirty-four years. At times it's been difficult, but I've learned from it all. This position and program would be a new emphasis, and I'm eager for that. My concern has been for the structures of oppression which hiddenly keep people knocked down. In terms of another strength and weakness, I am good at creating relationships. I mean that I tend to be out-going, have a good sense of humor, and am sensitve to people and their needs. I'm attracted to a lot of people. I'm a little afraid of that. In the past this has caused some difficulties. I'm looking forward to the work I would do with people of the neighborhood, to close supervision by you or another from the staff, and to teamwork with my fellow participants in this program. It will be a gift and also a challenge for me. I think I'll stop there.

Tomás: Well, thank you. Our staff was impressed with your application. In the light of this interview, I've been authorized by the staff to tell you that you will be informed about acceptance or rejection for the program within two weeks. I've enjoyed spending this time with you.

Sense of self

In the initial movement toward discipleship, the person feels poor yet desires to respond to the Lord. The person feels surprised at the call, yet senses that, indeed, there is a call. Knowing his own weakness and sinfulness, he wonders if he can respond and fears that he may not be able. He experiences a call to risk and to invest himself, trusting that the Lord will help. The process involves very much the acceptance of one's humanity: initially, the use of one's talents, as well as one's vulnerability and poverty, for the building of the Kingdom, and later the loving through pain, suffering, humiliation, and compassion.

Three things especially characterize the initial movement of the call to love: 1) an attraction into intimate relationship, either with the Lord, an individual, or a group; 2) a transparency in that relationship; and 3) an incipient vulnerability in one's humanity, which is linked to the intimacy and the transparency. Janet experiences all three movements.

The attraction toward this ministry surprises Janet. Yet it seems right to her despite her previous sense that it was meant for "stalwarts." She has wanted to do whatever the Lord wants and has developed her awareness of the needs of the poor. She really does not know whether she will succeed in this work or not, but she is willing to try. Encouraged by her pastor and trusting in the Lord, she is willing to risk.

Janet radiates a confidence that comes from her own sense of value as one loved by God. She is generous while willing to risk; she is fearful while willing to trust. She feels empowered despite her own sense of weakness and vulnerablity. She experiences a call to love in a new way and she senses that the Lord is loving her in giving her that call. She is experiencing the governing grace of being a loved and loving disciple.

The call to intimacy involves entrusting oneself to another transparently. Janet does not yet know the people, nor is she that accustomed yet to sharing her inner self. Yet in the interview with Tomás she is very open and honest. She shows good self-knowledge—aware of many of her gifts and some of her limitations. She is not afraid to deal with her weaknesses and hopes that she will be a freer person as a result. She handled herself quite well, although she said that she felt rather small and humbled.

The interview with Tomás represents the beginning of Janet's becoming more and more transparent and trusting in her relationship with the people. As she comes to know them more and more and tastes their goodness, their goodness will call forth her own goodness and humanity. She will risk her own person for them simply because she loves them. In this process she will become more vulnerable. She will probably become vulnerable in terms of people whom she knew before and do not now understand her behavior. This will be painful. But even more painful will be any misunderstanding that she experiences at the hands of the people toward whom she is growing in love.

Sense of the world

The loving disciple begins to see the importance of a concrete commitment to building a global society by acting at the local level. Having a deep sense of one's own self-worth, one feels with those who are deprived of their self-worth by an unjust situation. One feels called to change that situation, but it is a call that goes beyond some crusade or project or programs. Projects are secondary to the attraction to relationship. One fights for justice, yes; but it is the justice of concrete people whom he knows and touches. One simplifies his lifestyle because he does not want to take more than his share of the world's resources but even more so because he wants to experience a bond with people who have less. Relationship at a personal level with a particular community reflects itself in a greater attentiveness to the plight of human beings around the world. One keeps himself informed about what is happening in distant lands, somehow feeling more of a kinship with them. He makes contributions of prayer and almsgiving from this perspective.

Experience of God and prayer

Intimacy characterizes the nature of one's prayer as one grows as a loved and loving disciple. The intimacy is twofold: 1) increasing closeness to Jesus as a human person, a mysticism as one co-experiences the mysteries of Jesus' life; and 2) an increasing closeness with His people, especially the poor. Usually this closeness expresses itself in the form of a paradox, since one is initially much more aware of the separation and the desire for closeness than the actual experience of being close. Often, the person feels confused, aware of the fullness of God's love that has been lavished on him.

We shall pick up with Sr. Janet. She has been accepted into the program and has been working with the people of the neighborhood for the past eight months. Her ministry and the goodness of the people she is serving have begun to dominate her prayers. The following is an excerpt from her meeting with her spiritual director, Fr. Jack.

Jack: I'm happy we could meet.

Janet: There's so much to tell you and yet it's all very simple. I just love them. I'm beginning to take on their ethnic customs and ways of speaking. It's as if I've been introduced into family. I feel so alive. And I know it's the Lord gifting me.

Jack: You do seem brimming with vitality.

Janet: It's been wonderful, but not without moments of difficulty. In fact, there have been a few times when I wondered what I'd do next. We had one clash with the City Zoning Board where I feared that someone was going to get hurt. But my brothers kept their cool and didn't strike back. (laughing) You know, those situations get quite heated.

Jack: It sounds like they do. And you?

Janet: Oh, I've kept my cool. It's been easy. I was thinking . . . I feel as though I'm in love. I just see the goodness of each of the people that I'm working with. They are so good, so beautiful. Their struggles, their concerns, their fears. I've been there with them. And I laugh with them and sometimes I've cried with them. I've even prayed with them. I've felt so close to them. I think I'm becoming an Hispanic with them. It's been a total experience for me: the meetings, strategies, confrontations, picketing, publications. The whole thing of action and enablement has led me to parties, weddings, wakes and funerals, church processions. I think they look upon me as their sister or daughter.

Jack: It's complete, integral and, I gather, fulfilling.

Janet: Yes, very rich and satisfying. And the Lord seems so close. He's inside them and inside me. Oh, He's there at Mass, but that's like the naming of something that's already happened. They are so good. I know I just keep saying that over and over; it probably makes no sense. But God is so alive in them. I have been praying or at least trying to put time in every day. I wonder if it's prayer. I just think about the different people and thank Him for them and for the love that's inside me. It amazes me: these people are so simple and they are poor. I mean they've not had much education, at least not much that stuck. Yet they're wise in a profound way. And the way they party and joke and have fun. They really know how to laugh. Oh, I don't like all the drinking that goes on, and they are very loose with their bodies which at first scared me. But they respect me. I even sense that they protect me. How much the Lord is involved in all this, I don't know. Am I making sense?

Jack: Well, you put it well. You said that you feel as though you're in love. I sense that's true. And that you're experiencing what John meant in his first epistle when he wrote that God is love. Now you know what that means existentially, not just philosophically.

Janet: I really am in love, aren't I? Sometimes I think that it's all too good to be true. And then I remember that my parents are still not talking to me because of my involvement in this neighborhood. They are so filled with fear and prejudice. They don't understand. My sister wrote me last week and mentioned that Mom and Dad never talk about me. And that hurts. But I've got to live my life. I know deep inside that I belong here. But it's not without its pain.

Jack: I hear your sadness at your parents' silence and yet you are where you want to be. And so far it's been very good. You radiate life. And the Lord has blessed you with peace and a sense of bondedness with the people. Also with success, hey?

Janet: Yes, (smiling) it has been successful. The city has done an about-face and there has been progress. You can feel people pulling together. I just wonder how long this honeymoon will last.

Jack: Well, who knows. Thank the Lord for what is.

Union with God through union with His people characterizes Janet's prayer. The poor and the simple attract her. She focuses on them and their goodness. In the process her own goodness is being revealed and her identity with them, as well as her identity with Jesus. Yet she is not divorced from reality or from the pain of her life, e.g., the fears of confrontations and her parents' non-acceptance.

Passage to growth

The initial choice at this time in a person's growth in faith is that of transparency. Basically, the person chooses to accept and share his humanity—giftedness and weakness—with others in order to be in relationship and serve the Lord's people. Janet was very transparent in her initial interview with Tomás. Though she sensed her limitations, still she felt she could rely on the Lord's support in her work. She was also transparent with her spiritual director. In this situation, she shared her own gifts and her sense of being gifted. She experiences a call simply to be herself in whatever happens.

To some extent, she senses herself as being out on a limb, with a call to faith and trust. As one deepens trust in the Father and grows in intimacy with Jesus and His people, he grows accustomed to this poverty and vulnerability. Transparency crystallizes the heart of the initial movement of discipleship, simply because the person does not know where he is going. He feels out of control, yet drawn more and more into life. The image that he has of himself is purified; it no longer matters. His self gets lost in doing for the beloved.

The growth in discipleship becomes manifest as a person faces his reality and experience with the Lord. He seeks honesty and vulnerability as he struggles with the reality of his experience. He knows he may be hurt, but he has a sense that it will be worth it. He wants to do all for the beloved. Though he may feel very dry and poor and have a sense of his inability to love and to follow the Lord, deep down he still trusts that love can do these things.

The positive voices which nurture life and freedom call a person to foster relationship through being honest, human, and vulnerable. They call him to risk self-disclosure, both in word and in action. Frequently they call him to risk where he has not risked before, trusting that he follows the Lord and that the Lord will sustain him.

The negative voices undermine the person's sense of trusting in the Lord. They may tempt him to find God elsewhere than in the immanent Christ, for example, a transcendent God who appears apart from human reality and experience. Some of the unfreedoms dealt with in achieving one's identity may resurface again, e.g., the reliance on outside authority, feelings of inadequacy or guilt, fear of rejection, self-doubt, etc. Various rationalizations may occur which would foster one's keeping himself hidden and less vulnerable. The person may also seek to deny his call to share vulnerability or the other's call to accept that vulnerability.

B. THE COST OF DISCIPLESHIP (BELIEF IN JESUS AS STRUGGLING TO LOVE)

We pick up Sr. Janet two years later. She is upset and calls Fr. Jack on the phone.

Janet: Hello. This is Janet. (crying) I've got to talk to someone.

Jack: Well, I'm free for the next hour and a half. We can talk on the phone or you can come over.

Janet: I'll be over right away. Thank you very much.

(ten minutes later)

Janet: I'm sorry to be so upset, but I'm so grateful to you for seeing me right away. God's so good to let you be home and available.

Jack: You're upset. How can I help?

Janet: Well, first let me explain. (Blowing her nose and wiping away her tears. She lights up a cigarette.) It's just good to be here. (pausing) Simply put, I think I'm confused and hurt. This guy in the group, Eduardo, is very handsome and, I thought, a very fine man. Well, we've talked a good bit, usually about plans for mobilizing the unemployed in the neighborhood, and we've talked pretty late. He speaks about himself and gives me a big hug and a quick kiss at the end of our meetings, now that I think about it. But there's been nothing to it on my part. I mean I just love them all. Sure I like Eduardo, but no differently than the others. (The cigarette burns, untouched.) Evidently, some of the women saw us together several evenings in a row and began to talk. Finally, the gossip grew to the point that one of Eduardo's buddies asked him about how he felt toward me and Eduardo said that we had this intimate relationship and that he loved me and I loved him. It sounds so romantic: I don't know how he could say that; I've never treated him differently than the others. I do love him as a brother. And yet tonight I've been asking myself whether I've "turned him on" unknowingly. Am I really some slut who is just so warm and loving of everybody that she doesn't know what signals she's giving to others? I feel so confused. And I could blow it all, I mean the whole organization that we've built up. Everything's been moving according to plan until now. People are talking about pulling out. I feel humiliated before the group and thought ill of. And now it looks like the entire venture may fall apart because of the time I've spent with Eduardo. I feel that I've really messed it up. I thought I loved these people and they me, but now their criticism, their judgment, their rejection! It hurts. (crying) I didn't know where to turn.

Jack: Well, let's see if we can get some perspective on this. It hurts inside and your head is spinning. Is that right?

Janet: Yes. It really does hurt. I feel that I've loved too much. I've opened myself up to these people, honestly and freely, and now they are stabbing me. Yet, I cannot not love them. Even now. What's wrong with me? Am I crazy?

Jack: No, you're not crazy; but you are doubting yourself and your motives now that this pain has happened in your life.

Janet: I have been into self-doubt, haven't I? You know, if I had it all to do over again, I'd do it again. I cannot deny the great care I have for these people. It's a gift from the Lord. I know it, but I've been doubting it. It's been as if God's spirit is inside me loving, but I've doubted.

Jack: So, now you recognize that demon of self-rejection which would try to convince you that you were off-base from the beginning.

Janet: Yes (smiling). It's not the first time, though, is it? The pattern keeps repeating itself. I thought I was on top of it and had overcome it. Well, it's nothing like it used to be back in my twenties or when I was in high school. (pause) Also, I do love them, and it's a good love. But how could Eduardo say what he did?

Jack: Have you talked with him about this?

Janet: No.

Jack: Well, how do you know what he said? Perhaps you and he need to discuss what has been going on; and who said what; and what each meant; and how it was interpreted. In other words, some effective communication.

Janet: It seems obvious, as you say it. I recommend that to others so easily. I guess I'm just as human and just as poor as the next person. I can't see it when it's right in front of me. But what you say is right on.

Jack: And in terms of your relationship with the Lord, I encourage you to keep trusting in the movement from within, that sense of the Lord's spirit acting inside you. You may want to look at Luke 4 to see how Jesus was tempted and rejected while being led by that same Spirit. You are trying to follow in His footsteps—at least that's what I've heard you ask for.

You've wanted to love the way He loves. And so, it's happening. Be aware of the trap of self-doubt and the deception of non-communication. Your talk with Eduardo should clarify much for you. Okay?

Sense of self

The sense of life, intimacy, and exuberance in ministry may go on for some time. As Jack said in the conference two years earlier, in response to Janet's musing about how long the honeymoon will last, "Who knows? Thank the Lord for what is." Often enough, a traumatic event jars a person from the joy of intimacy and service. It is a temptation, just as Jesus was tempted in His search for the Father's will. It brings with it fear, confusion, and resistance as one faces the cost of loving.

An apparent miscommunication between herself and a fellow worker occasions Janet's temptation. We do not yet know what this will mean in the life of Janet. We have a sense that she has been growing in her love for the people and her desire to follow in the Lord's footsteps. Now the cost of loving and discipleship confronts her. In the face of unexpected rejection and misunderstanding, she is thrown into self-doubt, doubt of Eduardo's goodness, confusion about her minstry, and uncertainty about the people. She feels lost and uncertain how to proceed.

This experience signalizes a deeper movement in the life of the spirit, a movement which sorely tests a person's faith and commitment. At this time the person begins to feel much more deeply the cost of loving and of discipleship. He will experience new revelations of self-knowledge, especially new dimensions of self which he does not like. Janet will discover her fears, her resistance to risk, probably new dimensions of her own sexuality and her fear of them. She will be pushed to trust yet more radically in the Lord. She will doubt herself and her ministry even more. She will doubt whether the Lord is with her or even cares. These same experiences will also happen with regard to the people; she will doubt their love, acceptance, and care in the experience of being hurt, mis-understood, and rejected. Through these experiences the person is gifted with compassion which is at the heart of the person's ability to love.

Sense of the world

The dialogue does not dwell on Janet's sense of the world. Thus far she has felt the pain of the local people she has been working with and for and has worked to alleviate it. Now she is confronted with another source of pain: the immaturity of a co-worker, probably brought about in part by the conditions of social injustice. She struggles to continue to love the people, aware not only of how they have been sinned against, but also how their own sin can effect more sin. Not that this is at the forefront of Janet's consciousness. All she knows is that she wants to love and she wants to follow Jesus.

The temptation marks the beginning of the movement to the generative stage of development—where her fidelity to love leads her to embrace a societal and more global struggle for justice. Here her concern for others will reach beyond an interpersonal caring for a few to asking the hard questions about the root causes of injustice.

Experience of God and prayer

Janet has focused her prayer on Jesus and upon the Father. She has sensed herself as desirous of doing whatever the Father wants. She has also felt herself laboring at the side of Christ in the ordinary encounters of her day. Increasingly, she has striven to follow in the footsteps of the Lord through the Beatitudes, especially the Beatitude concerning poverty of spirit. She has felt poor especially in her risking herself in relationship, in her transparency (both in sharing herself and in being noticed), and in her honesty. Relationship has called her to this—her relationship with the Lord and with the people. She knows the Lord's love for her and for His people and feels called to love as He loves and to be His presence to these people. She has spoken the truth lovingly to them and expressed her own love for them truthfully.

She has prayed to be one with Jesus; but now she experiences pain, misunderstanding, humiliation, and rejection. As she brings these to the Lord, she knows that He too had these same experiences. Though she is confused and fearful, she still feels called to trust the Lord. She also feels called to continue to love the people in spite of their rejection and humiliation of her. With the aid of Jack, she claims the reality of her love for the people. Jack suggests that she contemplate the mystery of Jesus' being tempted in order to appreciate the present events of her life. She may also profit from praying the Passion.

Passage to growth

As one moves into deeper and deeper relationship with the

Lord and His people, all sorts of voices strive to get the person to withdraw from the commitment and relationship. The experience of being hurt and misunderstood can lead to resentment, revenge, and a what's-the-use attitude. The fear of being hurt can lead one to water down the truth of who he is or what he says. The fear of hurting the other may cause him not to confront or not to speak the truth that he feels in his heart. Put in psychological terms, the person may begin to protect himself through material possessions, through gaining control, and through independence. Fear underlies all three of these states: the fear of one's weakness, the fear of what others think or rejection, and the fear of investment in the other.

The voices toward freedom call the person to remain committed to the relationship through being honest, through going against the fears of rejection and of being hurt or hurting. They call the person to continue to express his love truthfully and to speak the truth lovingly. The person's vulnerability increases, yet love calls the person to continue to embrace vulnerability. The person is frequently called to forgive and to ask for forgiveness. This may take a very long time.

In the situation of Sr. Janet the negative voices strove to undermine the truth of who she has been in the community and to doubt herself, others, and the Lord. The positive voices have called her to continue commitment to honest relationship—in this situation, to honest communication with Eduardo.

C. THE PURIFICATION (BELIEF IN JESUS AS LOVING THROUGH SUFFERING)

We pick up Janet again, as the dying process continues. She

has seen Eduardo. A reconciliation might have happened, and Janet's participation in the Paschal Mystery might have stopped at this point without going deeper. Fuller participation in the Passion might have waited for another opportunity. Many never get this opportunity and others run from it once it is offered. We have chosen to have this mystery unfold further in Janet's life. Two weeks after her last conference she again calls Jack:

Janet: Hello. This is Janet again. (sobbing) I am sorry to bother you once more. But it is very difficult. Could I see you?

Jack: Janet, I'd like to be able to help; but I've got conferences lined up today back to back, and then I leave town for the week-end. The earliest we could get together would be on Monday.

Janet: (despondently) Well, it's like everything else. I don't want to wait, but I'll have to. Could we set a time for Monday?

Jack: How would 4:00 p.m. be?

Janet: Thank you very much. I really am grateful.

(A few days later, Monday at 4:00 p.m.)

Janet: I am very grateful that we could get together. How was your week-end?

Jack: Oh, it was fine. It was half-business and half-pleasure. It was good. How was yours?

Janet: Well, I survived. (crying) It really wasn't very good. I've had a very hard time. Could I tell you about it? (pausing, gaining control)

Jack: Please do.

Janet: I don't know where to begin. I've been trying to think how I could explain it to you, but I'm so confused. Let me announce the big news: I've been fired! It was ugly! I did see Eduardo as you had suggested and tried to initiate communication. I explained to him that I did care for him as a brother, but that I had heard that he felt differently towards me. Eduardo was silent at first and then exploded in anger at me. I couldn't believe it. He called me a "white bitch." It was then that I realized that I had hurt him—somehow. I still don't know how. Maybe I've been too open and said too much. I guess I had misled him unconsciously by my words and actions. It was a case of one person saying one thing and another interpreting it differently. Anyway, I did apologize to him. But he talked about the people in the neighborhood talking about and quoting me. At first I didn't understand what he meant. But then I realized that some of the older men as well as the women had picked up from a few things I had said that things were going on between Eduardo and me. It's all very confusing. In fact, they feared for other men like Eduardo. As if I were going to seduce them! I can't imagine how all this happened. I can't believe it. It's like a nightmare. Evidently after my session with Eduardo, several of the elders of the community met with him, and they decided to go to the program director and ask that I be let go. Sure enough, it worked. He called me in the next day, and after I explained what I thought had happened and my care for these people, he reminded me of our initial interview where I had spoken of my strengths and weaknesses. He pointed out that I had said that I am attracted to a lot of people and that I was afraid of that because in the past it had caused me some difficulties. Well, here it was causing difficulties again. I was floored! He said he could not risk my presence because he was trying to build community and not destroy it. He said that there was considerable hostility among the neighborhood toward me. (a long pause) So, I'm finished. I feel so cut off. It just hurts deeply. (weeping) What's wrong with me? This last week-end I thought I was going nuts. It was like I was losing my mind. I kept re-playing the scenario with Eduardo. I now see how wrong I was. I was just being myself but that was too much. And all the gossip; it makes me angry. I'm now the wicked witch. (more crying) I feel so alone. Even you went away this week-end. Alone and abandoned.

Jack: So, it's been and is extremely painful.

Janet: Yes, very painful. And there's nothing I can do to change things. I'm a laughing stock. And I hate it. I know it's my pride that's hurt. I've never been treated so rudely. My boss joined in on it too. I think I need a psychiatrist; I must be messed up—seducing others without even knowing it. (pause) But I went that route several years ago and learned that I'm just a warm person who is affectionate. Others judge that negatively. (lights a cigarette) How could all this have happened? How could God have permitted it? I don't understand it. (looking up to Jack, questioningly)

Jack: Well, you want to get on top of this and find answers to your questions. But you've not found any. Instead it's been embarrassing, alienating, and severely painful.

Janet: Yes. If all this was not so public it wouldn't hurt so much. I had the sense yesterday that I was stripped naked in front of the entire community and being nailed and lifted up—just like Jesus. What a trip! But that's what I felt like. This is Janet's crucifixion. And where in the hell is the Father! No wonder Jesus cried out "My God, My God, why have you forsaken me?" He's abandoned me, and so have my boss and those people whom I've loved. Only one difference between me and Jesus: it's my fault.

Jack: Oh?

Janet: Well, it is, isn't it? (pause, drawing on cigarette) But what could I have done differently? Really not much. Maybe I should never have taken the job in the first place. But it was so good. I really loved them. (looking up at Jack) I must be sick because I think I still love them, even with all this gossip and accusation. Even Eduardo, I hate him and I love him. He gets me so angry; he's such a little boy! But that's who he is. I can't change him. I must be a masochist. The Lord kept telling me: "Love my people." I wonder if that was all projection on my part. How many people hear the Lord saying things to them? I must be crazy. In fact, yesterday, I was wondering whether there is a God. Maybe I've been duped, and He's just a figment of my imagination.

Jack: So, now you are doubting everything: your work in the neighborhood, yourself, and even your God.

Janet: It is doubt, isn't it? The same damned doubt. But if I believe, then I am suffering like Jesus. Oh, I hate it!

Jack: Are you willing to undergo what Jesus experienced?

Janet: I've no choice. I can't erase what has happened. I've just got to die to my way of doing things. And I'm too powerless to do that; He'll have to do that in me.

Jack: Isn't He doing that now?

Janet (putting out cigarette): Okay. Yes He is. I don't like it. (I'm rebellious. I want it my way, but He's God. I hate all of this. Yet, we've gone too far. There's no turning back. Both He and I have risked too much. I don't know where I'll go next or what I'll do, but I cannot doubt the past, or myself, or Him. I wish it didn't hurt so much.

Sense of self

The essence of being a disciple is re-living the Paschal Mystery daily in one's life. A deep pain, hurt, and purification precede this process. The pain happens because one loves, because one chooses to remain faithful to relationship in spite of the hurt. Jesus experienced severe pain in the various dimensions of His Passion: physical abuse, psychological taunts, misunderstanding and outright hatred on the part of the religious leaders who should have recognized His message, betrayal by a trusted associate, flight on the part of his disciples, apparent abandonment by the Father, and self-doubt. The loved and loving disciple experiences many of these same hurts. He feels weak, helpless, and powerless in the face of circumstances which only get worse rather than better. All his efforts to save himself are rendered useless; he continues to be misunderstood and rejected. He finds himself more and more alone and unsupported. He fears annihilation. Often his sinfulness becomes much more manifest to him and probably to others; he is tempted to despair, to give up believing in self, in God, and in the power of love. He feels totally out of control of himself and of his world.

Janet has experienced a tremendous sense of darkness. All that she has recently known seems about to crumble—even her very self. She fears she is losing her mind: "Am I crazy?" She knows she has been striving to love; she knows, too, that she has tasted the goodness of the people and felt their love for her and the Lord's love for them. It seems inconceivable that love would not last. Yet it seems now destroyed and she wonders if it ever existed. She has a deep sense of her own failure; she has lost her job, but more than that she has lost the respect and the love of the people.

Janet had been trusting her sense of self and offering herself to the people. Increasingly, she became more and more vulnerable and shared the richness of her person with them. She felt the Lord calling her to this vulnerability. Now she experiences betrayal, rejection, and humiliation. Her pain makes no sense to her other than the fact that Jesus, too, walked a path filled with pain. But she hesitates to presume such identification with Jesus.

Sense of the world

In the process of purification the entire picture looms dark. The world kills, exudes violence and oppression, and treats people wrongly. We are all victims. We are all trapped. We all need a Savior.

This darkness is not always at the forefront of one's consciousness, as in the situation of Janet. The immediacy of her local situation blocks out much consciousness of the larger world; but, if the larger picture crashes in upon her consciousness, she would recognize the similarity to her own situation.

Pain permeates the purification process which leads to compassion. One's own sin and involvement in the unjust social structures become manifest in a new way. One senses himself trapped and powerless. He knows he needs a Savior. He knows we all need a Savior. There is no room here for defensiveness. Evil is pervasive. Love and goodness seem no longer possible. One's own suffering blends with the suffering of the poor and oppressed throughout the world. It unites him with Jesus—Jesus who walked this earth two thousand years ago, Jesus who lives and dies in His people today.

Experience of God and prayer

Prayer at this time can be very painful. The person experiences himself in the dark—groping, confused, abandoned by the Lord as much as by others. All he can do at this time is to be faithful to prayer and to relationship, even though it may appear so useless. If he becomes angry, he expresses that anger to the Lord. If one fears insanity or annihilation, he entrusts that to the Lord. He only experiences comfort in being with Jesus in His Passion, yet even this comfort seems a bit cold and intellectual due to this lack of positive feelings toward the Lord or toward His people. There seems to be no escape. As a person senses himself being out of control and even fearing annihilation, he hears the Lord say, "You must be; let go. Love them. I am enough. I will be your support." The person is aware of pain, knows he will hurt more, fears this and yet wants to be wherever the Lord is and wherever the Lord wants him to be. He experiences himself relying on God alone and becoming purified of all that keeps him from loving freely.

Passage to growth

The person feels himself called into deep intimacy with Jesus in His suffering and redemptive love of His people. He finds himself loving unconditionally; for, in the face of fidelity and commitment to relationship, he experiences only rejection and pain.

He experiences the same voices that we saw in the cost of discipleship. The positive voices urge increasing vulnerability and acceptance of pain. They call the person to forgiveness and to compassion and understanding of the other who has hurt and humiliated him. They call for fidelity to intimacy and relationship regardless of the cost.

The negative voices express themselves in the various fears, especially the fear of annihilation. The person fears that it is no longer his ego that is being annihilated, but his very self.

Self-doubt and self-pity increase, or at least the temptation to wallow in them. As one becomes even more aware of his sinfulness, he is tempted to self-condemnation and even despair. He experiences the desire to lash out and to rebel, and then almost immediately the urge to hide and to withdraw. He wants almost anything but real vulnerability in relationship. We notice Janet's struggle as she doubts herself; her anger at Eduardo practically overpowers her.

Freedom lies in death—death to the ego (although it feels like death to her very self). All along Janet had experienced little deaths (believing in her gifts, transparency, adapting to another culture, letting go the fears of her spontaneous affection, etc.); but now she experiences her greatest and most painful loss. She has lost her job, Eduardo, the community's respect. She has lost her desire to do something for the people. She has lost her self-confidence. There is nothing to cling to!

She becomes free only in embracing the pain and the rejection and in trusting the present moment of this passage through darkness.

D. THE LOVED AND LOVING DISCIPLE (BELIEF IN JESUS, THE HOLY SPIRIT, AND THE CHURCH)

The pain of the dying process continues until it is somehow transcended. This transformation and acceptance may happen gradually or suddenly. However it happens, it is experienced as a surprise and as a gift. We shall continue with the experience of Janet. Fourteen months have now elapsed since she was fired, and she now has another job in service of the poor. She has continued to see Jack monthly for spiritual direction. She has also made a directed retreat which was very painful; there she accepted her experience of trying to enable the community and her failure in that attempt. She has grown in further self-knowledge. Below is an excerpt from another conference in spiritual direction:

> Janet: My prayer this month took an interesting turn. I thought you'd like to hear about it. My new job for the government on communications with the marginated on the near west side has continued to go well, but about three weeks ago I had a phone call from one of the new leaders in the old neighborhood where I had all the trouble.
>
> Jack: Oh?
>
> Janet: Yes. Well, we decided to have lunch downtown together. But he showed up with three others. And they were there to ask my advice. And one of them was Eduardo's younger brother.
>
> Jack: So, some memories from the past revisited?

Janet: Not exactly. I mean, I didn't know what they wanted. And as they spelled it out, I began to see that here I was doing enablement but from afar. They were discussing the formation of a new coalition, with a broader base among the people. But it was just so good to be with those people again. They really are so good and so lovable. So, I tried to listen to their desires for a new alliance and fed back to them the goals they seemed to be articulating. (smiling) You know how they articulate goals: with all that fervor and with those big eyes opened wide. I loved every minute of it. We laughed and had a wonderful time together. Lunch lasted almost three hours.

Jack: It sounds like a pleasant surprise.

Janet: Yes, it was. Very pleasant. And since then, almost daily they come up in my prayer. I have the sense of being hidden and of delighting at what is happening in their community. They are such good people! I'll always love them, but now there is a new freedom in me. I'm not clingy. They are still His little ones. And in their humor, the way they tell stories—they're wonderful. I don't know if this coalition will work out. But that's not all. Last week, they wanted to get together again, so I thought: why not have the four of them over for supper. So that's what we did. It was less formal, less business, more just being together. Oh, we did our work, but afterwards we sat around and told stories until the wee hours of the morning. (pauses) In my prayer, I've had a sense of the Lord living in them, in the leadership and in the grassroots of the community. I sense He is laboring within them. He is so very much there. At times in my prayer, I've been very consoled at what is happening in those beautiful little ones of His. At other times, I wonder if it's real; if what's happening now is more of my imagination. By and large, I've believed that it is Him. And I've seen my call to be with His people in the little things, hidden, and especially with people like Al. Incidentally, although Al's weak with cancer at this point, he is on the coalition leadership. God chooses the weak. It's amazing.

Jack: The Lord is manifesting Himself to you in and through others, especially the *anawim*. You see Him at work in them. Yet you still are called to faith and to set aside your unbelief.

Janet: Yes, He wants me to live in faith. And not to doubt. I'm learning. (laughs) Then there is Eduardo's little brother. He *is* little: five-feet-six! They call him Bennie. Bennie's almost twenty-one and is filled with all the enthusiasm that Eduardo had. But he is clear about what he sees the needs of the area to be, and he's a little tiger. Somehow we hit it off very well. I think he respects me. And, frankly, that helps after what I've been though with his brother. By the way, Eduardo's living in Canada now, doing lumber work out west. Bennie has vision. He's tasted poverty and knows that the lack of jobs, the drop-outs from school, and drug abuse are key problem areas. He's organized the old gangs to do volunteer work in the neighbor-hood. They are protecting the people, especially the youngsters. So, the scene is very hopeful, and I'm involved, but not in any way I would have imagined a couple of years ago. I'm amazed at how peaceful and even joyful I am. There is a paradox or mystery in all this. It just isn't the way I thought it would be. But it is very good. I really believe that it is Him.

Jack: Well, enjoy it. Live it. Believe.

Let us proceed to reflect on what has happened.

Sense of self

Having passed through the darkness and pain of the dying process, Janet now has a much more sober sense of herself and of reality. She still exudes enthusiasm and delight in the goodness of the people, but her joy is much more subdued as she deals realistically with the people who enter her life. She knows that the hollowing out has been a blessing; she has reconciled herself with the past pain and realizes that further pain will come. She can listen and respond to the needs of the people without expectation of return, without the desire to be accepted in the process, or without the need to be in the limelight. Her relationship with the people continues or is born again. She does not have the satisfaction that she originally hoped for, but she knows that the relationship has been purified and that this new relationship is far richer. No longer does she project her own needs on the community, but she accepts the people as they are much more freely.

Once the person has been so purified, he can love compassionately without counting the cost. He can console, reach out to others, and be with them in their experience without any desire for recompense. The person experiences a new maturity and wisdom concerning life's processes. He knows that the meaning of life is contained in loving, and that loving means entering the world of the other in selflessness. The past pain has been healed, though he still feels vulnerable. He knows he will experience pain again, but now the pain is different. This pain comes from suffering with the other. Before he experienced a private pain caused by one's ego being in the way; now he senses deeply an inner freedom. He is willing to risk hurt and pain again, for he only wants to love. He knows further that the ability to love is a gift and that without the Lord and His power he cannot love, but with His aid he is confident in his ability to love. He experiences a freedom to love more truthfully and compassionately. When the door is barred to deeper relationship, the person puts himself in the other's circumstances and forgives. He no longer wants to run away. He senses being in the Lord's presence, though at times this sensing can be elusive.

Sense of the world

After a person has been hollowed out in the purifying process, he knows the pervasiveness of social evil and encounters it in a variety of circumstances. Thus Janet moves on to a new job, but still remains active in working for justice. She has become much more a citizen of the whole world.

As one grows in the capacity to love, which involves not just a doing for but also a being for, he becomes more and more a world citizen. He becomes eager for enablement, empowerment of others, and the freedom of the other—even if it means pain for himself. He becomes a person of compassion, willing to do for, to be with, and to suffer hardship, loss, and rejection for the opportunity of loving deeply. Thus Janet has risked again in taking on a new job. She has also risked being hurt again in getting involved with the people in the neighborhood. She has a much greater sense of perspective now as she deals with the people. She has owned her own previous sin in her relationship with them. She also is aware of their sinfulness and potentiality for sin. But love calls her again into relationship with them. She has moved beyond the romantic level of love to a more mature form of love which has passed through the stage of disillusionment in love. She desires union—a union which recognizes sin, humanity, and the cost of loving.

Experience of God and prayer

The person develops a sense of finding God in all things in his prayer. He sees the Lord in every experience: in the joys, in the sorrows, in the hopes, in the fears. The Lord has created and is now creating anew. The person senses himself co-laboring and co-creating with God and feels a quiet joy and peace in doing so. He senses himself as the Lord's presence.

The person may experience some of the gifts of the Holy Spirit. These graces are less ecstatic and accompany the quiet willingness to be a channel of grace for others. It is not that pain is absent from the person's life. No, the person continues to live the Paschal Mystery, while recognizing the Lord's fidelity in all the pain. He endures in hope.

Transparency also continues, but the person more easily overcomes his fears of openness. The Lord is Lord of all; not to be transparent is to distrust his Lordship.

It is the vulnerability that takes on a new tone—less one's own and much more the care and concern for the wounded and poor of this world. The person knows that he, too, is weak, vulnerable, and a sinner; but these do not matter anymore. The person feels with others in their pain.

Janet speaks of how she senses the Lord at work in the people of her former community. She is consoled by His presence there and is content to accompany them in a much less spectacular way than before. Yet she knows her help is more effective and real. At times she doubts her experience and is tempted not to believe, much as the disciples continued to doubt the presence of the Lord after His Resurrection. But she recognizes her call to believe, and she is joyful about this challenge.

Passage to growth

At this stage of growth a person deeply desires to radiate the joy of the Risen Lord and hope in His fidelity. The struggles—the negative and positive voices—that have been in a person's life still continue, but they have less power to throw the person off the path of the Lord. He feels anchored at his center, knowing that the Lord is faithful and will continue to be faithful no matter what the experience.

Janet has plenty of data on which to base her trust. Her initial call to the poor has continued in her new job. The call to that specific community has changed, but she knows her new form of hidden presence is much deeper and much more enriching. She has let go of her own personal needs and desires and has become a much more enabling presence. She experiences Bennie's role in leadership as a special gift; he has all Eduardo's natural gifts and attractiveness, together with a maturity rooted in his vision of the needs of the community.

As Janet struggles to believe that the Lord continues to work in her and in the community, the negative voices call her to mistrust and doubt her experience. Now she more easily recognizes them and can deal with them.

Summary

We have seen the process in which Janet has grown in belief in Jesus. She has grown in trust, transparency, and vulnerability. She has grown in intimacy and generativity; she has developed her sense of mission and her ability to carry out that mission effectively.

The grace of mission comes after one has a sense of his identity and of his being loved uniquely by God. It also comes after one knows that he is loved as a sinner. Because of her awareness of her own sinfulness as well as her sense of the awesomeness of the task of working with the poor, Janet was humbled by the possibility of her new call; yet she could claim the gifts she brought to the job.

In using her talents with the people, she discovered herself growing closer to them. She was bonded to them through this trust and transparency. Even her weaknesses became a source of union. Eventually, *who she was* got in the way of her mission—not so much by her own doing but through the sinfulness of the situation. The immaturity of Eduardo and the lack of freedom in the people led to a rejection of what seemed to her to be her own goodness and being. In the face of this experience, Janet was tempted to doubt herself, the people, and God. Janet resisted the temptation, accepted the further revelation of her own and the people's sinfulness, let go her own needs and desires, and accepted humbly and sadly her dismissal from the job. But she made the significant choice to continue to be faithful to the poor in spite of the pain. This choice led to new life not only in her new situation, but also in the previous situation. In the process she found herself experiencing the various mysteries of Jesus' life.

10

THE SPIRITUAL DIRECTOR'S FACILITATION OF BELIEF IN JESUS AND APOSTOLIC COMMITMENT

In the initial movements of growth in discipleship the director simply companions the person, accepting whatever dimensions of his humanity the person comes in touch with and chooses to communicate. He functions mainly as an accepting listener as the person chooses to be vulnerable and transparent.

If the person experiences dryness in prayer, which frequently may happen, the director can call him to faith, as well as to the awareness that he cannot manipulate the Lord. Most probably, the person is praying for the experience of whatever the Lord wants, but will not have anticipated dryness as the Lord's response. It will probably prove useful if the director helps him integrate this experience into the pattern of spiritual growth that has been going on in his life.

The director fosters whatever helps the person accept and communicate his humanity. The director calls him to be truthful and loving in relationship. Such a posture, of course, presumes that the director himself is comfortable with intimacy and relationship. St. Ignatius wisely states that one should direct another only in the stages that he or she has some experience of. If the director himself has not experienced some degree of intimacy with God and transparency in relationship, he will become frightened of the level of communication that the directee has.

As the person grows in relationship with the Lord and his sense of discipleship deepens, the director often fades more into the background. The Spirit is obviously leading and in control. The director's main task is simply to accompany the person in the process of growing intimacy with the Lord and His people. Often he says very little, but simply manifests his faith. The book depicts this kind of situation in the first session between Jack and Janet. Janet exudes life and enthusiasm about her contact with the people. She senses herself falling in love with them. Jack simply savors her joy and enthusiasm, encouraging her to enjoy the gift of God's consolation as long as it lasts. Jack knows that there will probably come a time when Janet's joy and enthusiasm will be tested.

When the experience of temptation happens and the vulnerability and intimacy of the relationship are threatened, the director may take a more active role. We saw Jack do this when he called Janet to get an objective view of what had been the nature of her relationship with Eduardo and with the community. He encouraged her to speak honestly with Eduardo and to give him a chance to clarify what he was doing and saying. Most importantly, the director helps the person sort out the voices that lead to life and those that lead to death and helps uncover the patterns in these voices. Jack unmasks the demon of self-doubt and self-rejection that Janet had seen in her life before and had been able to resist in the past. With this help, Janet accepts her own love for the people. She also owns her own humanity and vulnerability, which opens her to accepting more fully the vulnerability and humanity of Eduardo and the people. The director calls the person to deeper relationship and vulnerability, urging him not to yield to the fears and hurts or to the voices of inadequacy. The director manifests faith in the belief that the mystery of God is present in the fidelity to relationship in spite of the pain.

Here it is crucial that the director understand what is happening from his own experience. Faced with the pain of the directee, he will be tempted to protect him and to rescue him from the depths of vulnerability. He can remind the person that he is free to say "no" at any time, but he himself should not try to take the pain away.

Often enough, the explicitation of patterns can prove helpful. The director points to the life and experience of Jesus. Here the person discovers the pattern of Jesus—poverty, powerlessness, and trust as opposed to security, power, and control. The person gradually comes to understand the Lord's way, to choose that way, and to be so close to Jesus that he also *feels* that way. Thus Jack suggests that Janet might find the temptations of Jesus (Luke 4) a suitable place to pray.

As the pain deepens, it becomes all-pervasive. The director helps the person connect his spiritual life with the rest of his life (his job, other relationships, etc.). These situations, too, will often seem empty and fruitless. Even the relationship with the director enters in. The person will frequently express anger toward the director. Again, the director may be tempted to rescue the person from the pain and darkness rather than let the person receive the death the Lord is bringing.

The person wants to end the pain and, at the least abatement, will judge it is over. The director encourages further waiting. He allows the person's resistance to be further broken down. His chief tasks are simply to be present, to witness and to acknowledge the pain, to wait in faith with the directee, and to encourage trust of the process. He may suggest Scripture passages dealing with the Lord's Passion and calls the person to focus upon the Lord; he may suggest more time alone in the Garden. The Psalms of distress illumine the situation. Focus upon the desire to love the whole Christ is usually helpful. The director can remind the person that he is free to end all this and that he does not have to love or to stay in the situation, but the director knows that the person wants to love no matter what the cost.

Frequently, the director simply accompanies (the way Mary and John did at the foot of Jesus' cross). Jack asks Janet: "Are you willing to undergo what Jesus experienced?" He elicits faith and trust in the Lord, "Isn't He doing that now?" Janet believes, though her faith is being stretched. The process reveals more of her sin. She has no one to cling to except the Lord. The pain hurts and cannot be stopped. Here Jack's tone of voice or facial expression can be the place where he either accompanies Janet or abandons her. If the director has gone through the dying process himself, he will have the freedom to be compassionate.

The final death happens at the Lord's pace, as does the Resurrection. When the person experiences the joy of loving and enabling after having passed through a deep purification process, the director has only a minor role to play. He simply encourages the person to live his experience, to trust it, and to be grateful for it. Appointments may become less frequent;

and, when they happen, the director may find himself as a joyful witness to the action of grace and, perhaps, as a sounding board. Subsequent crises and temptations are less traumatic than the first time for the individual, for he has traversed this ground before. The director calls the person to faith and to trust what he knows and has experienced of the Lord. Remembering is very important. The director can help the person face the present by recalling past events and patterns of the Lord's presence in his life. The Eucharist serves as a focal point where the person celebrates that he continues to live the Paschal Mystery and that the victory has been won.

CONCLUSION

This book has focused on the process of growth in faith, emphasizing the governing grace at a particular stage of development. The book paints the picture "abstractly" and in a linear fashion. Individual persons, of course, are not abstract. No person will actually fit this mold; and, in fact, the stages overlap. Growth is more cyclical than linear. The person grows dynamically. Issues more properly raised at one stage of development recur again at a later stage, but in a slightly nuanced fashion. This book does not capture these nuances and treats the stages more "purely." God's grace is always offered. Patterns will be similar and old weaknesses may show themselves in new circumstances; but something new is happening in the life of a person.

What is new? The person, the face of God, the way of praying, the sense of the world, the freedom to be discovered, the quality of action, the capacity for union with God. Because of these shifts the person's spirituality may change, as well as the interpretation of events and feelings. The same behavior has a different significance depending on the developmental growth of a person.

This chapter will tie together the development that has gone on in the person through the successive stages. It will also show how the role of the director changes and give some guidelines for the discernment of spirits.

Sense of self

We have seen several movements through the lives of a few people: Phil, Teresa, Betty, Pete, Mark, Shirley and Janet. We could have traced the growth in faith of the same person through the various stages of freedom. It seemed, however, that a variety of personalities might prove more helpful. Now let us tie these together.

a) Sense of one's uniqueness

Phil, Teresa, Betty, and Pete all do not yet have a fundamental sense of self. All struggle toward the gift of believing in their own goodness and accepting being loved. None of them has a sense of his own inner authority or uniqueness; each places his authority outside himself. Phil especially is caught in his generalizations; he judges everyone to be of the same mold, i.e., like himself. All of them want to be accepted by others and have difficulty standing apart and making a choice which might displease the significant people in their lives: God as Judge or hierarchical Church (Phil and Teresa), one's immediate relationships (Betty), one's father (Pete).

Mark is growing in the sense of his own uniqueness. He has begun to relish his own goodness and individuality with some degree of trust. Each experience opens him up to a sense of his competence and worthwhileness; thus he is growing in self-confidence. He accepts his own growth and he is eager to grow more.

Though Shirley seemed secure in herself and in her abilities, the dawn of darkness began to undermine her security. She continually tried to remedy the darkness, using all her skills and power to change the situation. Eventually, she realized through grace that she cannot save herself and that God freely chooses to save her. This was a rich experience of her own uniqueness. She recognized it as a sign of special love from God to be loved in the darkness and in her own weakness and sinfulness.

Janet's sense of her own uniqueness goes beyond that of Mark and Shirley. Not only does she know herself as good and lovable, but she feels a unique mission to love others. She comes to accept the pain involved in loving as a further sign of God's special love for her and of the unique way in He calls her.

b) Focus

Those without a sense of self (Phil, Teresa, Betty, and Pete) focus primarily on themselves and their own needs and desires because they are fundamentally unsure of themselves. They lack the self-confidence necessary for truly altruistic behavior. Even Phil whose actions can appear very generous and self-sacrificing, is really only satisfying his innate need to feel that he is good through following the law and measuring up to his own ideals.

Mark and Shirley also focus on themselves, but they have a true sense of themselves as seen in God's eyes. Shirley's sense of self is fuller than that of Mark's, since she is gaining an appreciation of her own sinful nature and grows to be at peace with her sinfulness in the presence of the Lord.

Janet's focus is different. She focuses outward, on mission. In the process, of course, she learns more about herself which she values and experiences as a grace. But her purpose and focus are not to learn more about herself. She wants to help others come to a knowledge and love of themselves and of God and to help build the kingdom together with them.

c) Sense of inner life

Phil, Teresa, Betty, and Pete have little appreciation for their own inner life. They have not yet claimed their real selves. Rather than look to their own inner being, they focus on their own behavior. They frequently compare themselves to others, wondering if they measure up. Phil, Betty, and Pete have constant radar out to detect whether or not they are liked and accepted. Teresa gains "acceptance" through superficial joys, e.g. her work in the parish. Both Betty and Pete generally judge themselves as disliked or, at least, worry about being disliked. Phil is less controlled by the desire to be liked, since he has generally repressed or suppressed his feelings in favor of doing what he thinks is right.

Mark, Shirley, and Janet are much more attuned to their own inner life and eager to explore it. Shirley finds the process of opening up to the negative in her life very difficult and painful. Though she resists the process, she ultimately chooses to be faithful to self-exploration. Janet rests more comfortably than either of the other two in being open to self-discovery, though she, too, experiences pain in being vulnerable. She possesses a deep-seated peace in the fidelity of the Lord's love in her life that roots her growth in self-knowledge.

d) Coping with ideals

Phil, Betty, and Pete have very high ideals. Phil has idealized his sense of self and generally succeeds in obeying the law. When he finds that he fails to live up to his ideals, he resolves to try harder. Betty and Pete also have high ideals; but, unlike Phil, they find themselves not measuring up to these ideals. Pete is growing in his ability to accept his inability to measure up; Betty may never do so.

Because of their idealism they demand much of themselves. They also demand much of others. Phil is generally frustrated and angry at the inability of others to live up to his ideals and can be quite intolerant of failures. Betty and Pete make different demands on others. Since they do not yet value themselves, they possess strong and excessive needs for affirmation. Eventually, their friends may refuse to meet their unrealistic needs.

Mark and Shirley also have to cope with idealism in their lives. The thorn of idealism pricks Mark from time to time, but it is not at the essential cutting edge of his growth. It is, however, in the life of Shirley. As Shirley copes with the negative and sin in her life, she is being weaned of the idealized image that she has had of herself. This weaning is very painful, for the idealized self-image dies hard.

Janet also is being pruned of her false ideals, but she does not experience the same wrenching that Shirley does. Her own humanness continually confronts her, but she generally accepts her weaknesses peacefully. As she progresses in her ability to be vulnerable, she desires less to protect herself by yielding to false ideals.

e) Acceptance of feelings

One cannot claim himself without honestly owning his feelings. Until writing in her journal, Teresa had been unreflective of her feelings and unable to nuance and say "no" to them. Often the person of whim expresses surface feelings and seems incapable of much depth. Phil, Betty, and Pete tend to suppress feelings or to dwell unhealthily in negative ones such as self-pity. Phil relies almost exclusively on his reason and tends to debunk feelings, affectivity, and intimacy. He regards feelings as temptations. Betty basically does not like her feelings and thus often gets upset with them and with herself. Pete is gradually learning to cope with his feelings and accept them with varying degrees of success. Mark will grow insofar as he can enter into and savor his feelings, especially the positive ones of joy and gratitude. Shirley must enter into her negative feelings, especially anger and hurt, and then allow these to become revelative of God and of herself. Janet is called to trust her feelings, especially those of love and compassion, and allow them to influence her apostolate. In the initial moment of becoming a loved and loving disciple, one facet of the risk of vulnerability is the sharing of feelings, which comprises part of the path to growth in intimacy and love. The cost of discipleship also often involves an honest acceptance and communication of feelings. The gift of discernment also involves trust of one's feelings.

Sense of the world

Teresa had very little sense of the world or of people's needs. Her focus had been on herself and her own pleasures. She was no longer a person of principle; she had been settling her problems by yielding to her own whims or to the desires of others. After her retreat, she feels the need to be more responsible in her relationships.

Phil, Betty, and Pete are more apt to have a sense of justice and of the rights of others. They are moved by "rights" and a sense of fairness. Though we did not really see in their dialogues their sense of justice, they may feel guilty in the face of injustice, since they value highly their sense of what is right. Unfortunately, they do not nuance or distinguish among various rights and various truths. What surfaces as justice for one person may not necessarily embody justice for another person. Their "objectivity" needs to be tempered by the subjectivity of a personal relationship.

The person of principle often masks a hidden anger. He tends to be defensive, often rationalizes, and can lay 'trips' on others. We saw these tendencies in Phil's Sunday sermon. Almost always when the person of principle speaks about justice, the audience experiences an irrational guilt. Phil uses the church law to lay guilt trips upon the people. The person of principle is generally a kind person who would do anything in his power to help you except allow you to break the law. He is not really a compassionate person who understands and feels the complexity of motivation and of the human situation.

Mark, Shirley, and Janet do have a sense of their own person and can begin to entrust their person to others and to God. In so far as Mark and Shirley accept themselves and their own goodness, they too have a deep sense of what is right and what is wrong. However, unlike Phil who roots his values in a sense of the law, Mark and Shirley value the equality of all people as created uniquely and lovingly by God. They have a vague sense of their own universal identification with men and women throughout the world. Neither knows what to do about injustice. Because Mark is in touch with his own goodness and does not appreciate his own sinfulness, he tends to be naively optimistic about how to combat injustice. Full of enthusiasm, he responds generously to immediate needs. He cannot address the larger global needs, where his naivete becomes especially evident.

Shirley, too , does not really know how to respond to injustice. The vague relationship to others that Mark and Shirley feel influences their sense of justice, but Janet's sense of justice is much more consciously based on relationship. In the early stages of working with people, her closeness to them leads her to feel and suffer with them. Her heart is moved; she is sympathetic and empathetic. At first she involves herself locally with a few people and sacrifices little things for them. Though open to understanding the complexities of unjust social structures, she takes a certain "band-aid" approach to immediate needs and suffering. This immediate response is a necessary developmental stage with regard to effecting justice. Unless one's heart is moved by personal interaction with the people, one cannot combat the evil of social structures with the necessary compassion for oneself and for others.

The longer Janet remains affectively bonded to the people the more she asks the hard questions about the injustice of an oppressive culture, and economy, and of social structures which foster poverty, create dependence, and stifle freedom, dignity, and creativity. Once Janet has been hurt by the people and still chooses to remain committed to them, her capacity for loving sacrifice is even greater. Not only does she sacrifice her own time and energy, but she lets go her own feeling of power, her own culture, her own rights and needs, even her own sense of the self she knew and valued. Janet achieves the essence of Christian morality which goes beyond strict justice and calls us to love others not according to their rights but in terms of their needs regardless of the cost to ourselves.

Experience of God and prayer

As we look at the development of relationship with God,

several areas seem important to focus on: the sense of God's providence, the sense of God's attitude towards behavior, the relationship to Jesus, and the nature of one's prayer. All of these areas change, as one grows in faith.

a) Sense of God's providence

Phil, Teresa, Betty, and Pete do not have a full sense of God being personally and lovingly involved in their lives. God looms all-perfect and demanding. Teresa feels that God has punished her for her breaking the law; she fears drawing near to Him. Phil and Betty experience God as impersonal and withdrawn; insofar as they sense Him personally involved in their lives, they picture Him as a demanding Judge who never seems satisfied despite all their efforts. Phil has grasped intellectually that God is a loving Father, but he has not yet begun an affective relationship with Him. Pete is beginning a personal relationship with God, but still vacillates.

As a person claims his self and his own identity, he moves from a sense of God as impersonal to a sense of God's personal love and concern. Mark experiences God as an all-pervasive loving Creator. God constantly calls him to enjoy life and pursues him with His love. To a certain extent, Shirley also experiences God's pursuit. Beneath her unpleasant experiences of herself and the world lies a quiet abiding belief that God is active in this negative experience and pain and that He is somehow revealing Himself and sharing Himself with her, even though she does not feel it. Janet rests easily with the idea of God's constant love and presence and strives to recognize His voice at all times.

b) God's attitude toward behavior

Before one senses his self and his own uniqueness, he

focuses on his own behavior, striving for the ideal and avoiding sin. His image of God correlates to this focus.

Phil, Teresa, Betty, and Pete all see God fundamentally as a Judge, and especially as a Punisher, who is very concerned about their behavior. Teresa is generally unreflective and sees God as someone in control of her life and its circumstances; she claims no responsibility for herself. Though she would like to think of God as being quite tolerant of her, in her more serious moments she fears that God will punish her.

Phil, too, is riddled with fear. He constantly strives to do right lest he be punished for doing wrong. Because he generally does the good, he expects to be rewarded for his actions. Betty and Pete also want to do what is right and fear doing wrong; however, since they generally focus on the negative, they expect to be punished for their misbehavior.

Prior to claiming one's identity, a person's behavior looms very large in his own eyes as well as (he thinks) in the eyes of God. After claiming identity, one's focus shifts from behavior to being. Thus it seems to Mark that he can do no wrong. He immerses himself in action, being, and life. He views everything as a gift from God. He seeks to enjoy the world and to be thankful. The situation is quite nuanced for Shirley. She struggles with her own behavior. She eventually recognizes her own sin and sinfulness. When she strives to change, she discovers that her own behavior cannot undo her sin. As long as she concentrates on her own behavior and judges that God does the same, she is stuck. In this process she reverts to previous images that she has had of God—a Judge, or an impersonal force who controls all but does not care enough to heal the evil in her and in the world. Her freedom lies in her discovering that God is less concerned with her behavior and more concerned with her coming to Him and her being in relationship with Him.

Janet focuses on living—on being in relationship and carrying out that relationship in her deeds. She knows that God is, indeed, concerned with her behavior; but she senses that the action itself is less important. What matters is the relationship and the attitude of love she manifests in her choices. Thus, painfully, she can move on to a new job. She can also forgive those who hurt her in her former job.

c) Relationship to Jesus

Prior to the claiming of identity and to an experience of personal communication with God where one accepts His love, a person views Jesus as an all-perfect model to be imitated. Jesus, then, for the person of principle, exemplifies the law in the form of a person; as such He really functions as an abstract value rather than as a loving person. Because the person of principle covets generosity and sacrifice, he very often views Jesus as the one who accepted the cross and suffering. Thus we see Phil telling his congregation that his "cross" is to honestly tell the people what is right and not to "soft-pedal" the law.

Mark relates to God as a loving Father and Creator rather than to the person of Jesus. In so far as Jesus might enter into his prayer, He appears as the Lord of the Universe or of all things. Shirley, too, relates to God as Father and Creator. However, in the depths of her pain and struggle she looks to Jesus on the cross. Eventually, she relates to Jesus as the powerful Savior in her life, though she really does not yet know who He is or feel an interpersonal love for Him. She knows that Jesus has died on the cross to free her from her sins. After the experience of her healing, she wants to grow in relationship to Him.

Janet is developing an interpersonal relationship with the human Jesus. As she claims her own humanity and vulnerability, she grows in the awareness of Jesus' own humanity and vulnerability. She increasingly feels identified with the human Jesus portrayed in the Gospels and senses herself reliving the mysteries of His life; this feeling of identification brings her great consolation and strength. She is growing in her relationship with Jesus as a friend and companion. She also is becoming more aware of Jesus as being present in the poor; and, as she grows in love for them, she knows she is growing in love for Him.

d) Nature of prayer

Prior to claiming one's identity, one's personal prayer is characterized by petition and meditation. Phil, Betty, and Pete reflect a lot on life and use this examination of conscience as an important form of prayer. They also like to meditate. When they are thinking, they generally do not know if they are talking to themselves or to God. Generally, they expect to have God as a part of their lives; so , even if prayer does not seem fruitful, they often judge that they ought to pray and therefore try to do so. In times of need, they, too, petition God's help.

Mark's, Shirley's, and Janet's prayers are more characterized by informal conversation, by praying from their heart, and by a familiar relationship with God. Mark often prays in gratitude and praise, as he rejoices in the gifts and beauty of this life and of the Lord's love. Shirley's prayer often seems dry and difficult. When she speaks with God, she often shares her negative feelings. Thus she complains, whines, begs, and demands in the process of being pruned of her desire for consolation and in the discovery of her own sinfulness and her powerlessness to free herself from it. Her prayer before Jesus on the cross can be very genuine and filled with sorrow for her sins and later gratitude for His mercy.

Janet prays much more calmly, though at times she prays quite passionately. Prayer of the imagination or the contemplation of the Gospels helps deepen her sense of identification with Jesus. As she grows in her ability to discover God in all things, much of her prayer focuses on the desire to recognize the Lord's presence in her life. She often contemplates God present in the people and brings the people before God in her prayer.

The exprience of choice

People often come to a spiritual director because they want to make a choice or a decision, in which they desire to "do God's Will." People face a lot of possible concrete decisions: change of residence, change or choice of career, change of lifestyle, returning to a foreign culture, returning to an old ministry, use or non-use of one's talents, deepening or severing a relationship, choice of vocation, how to use money or time, and so on.

Though the person questions a specific decision with a given content, the specific content is *not* the important matter. What is important is the growth in faith that happens in the process of decision-making. God uses the occasion of a decision to spur the person on to further development. A particular decision surfaces the present call to personal growth or the governing grace that is now operative within a person. The process of decision-making in a Christian context is called discernment.

The basis of Christian discernment is an ignorance that

produces strong feelings. One does not know what God wants, but one *desires* to know. Faced with a decision, the person experiences strong contradictory feelings, some of which ally themselves with freedom, growth, and relationship to God and others of which embody death and stagnation. A conflict occurs deep within the person at the core of his being. Hence, the big hassle. More is at stake than just this action or this specific decision. Some of the feelings appeal to one's strength and one's deepest self; these call to life and growth. Others embody fears, doubts of self, others, and God, feelings of inadequacy and guilt, worries about what others think, and making comparisons. These lead to non-life and a failure to grow.

The nature of the discernment depends on the level of personal and spiritual growth that the person has achieved. Teresa ordinarily makes her decisions in terms of what she likes and what she does not like. She chooses to do what brings her up and avoids what brings pain and punishment. She is very dependent on what others think. If she is in a good mood, she is apt to be quite generous; if she is angry, she will probably explode. Such a pattern of life is appropriate for a five-year-old, but it is very inappropriate and non-life-giving in a thirty-nine-year-old.

Though growth for the person of whim can happen gradually through a normal developmental cycle, it is generally some traumatic event that spurs the person to constructive action. The voice of the Lord for the person of whim leads him to put discipline into his life. Teresa decides to face honestly with her husband her pain about her son.

Phil, however, is quite disciplined. Discipline, in fact, keeps him from further growth. The voice of life (or the "good spirit") leads Phil to let go his ideals and his need to control and to act more spontaneously. He needs to express his feelings, enter into relationships, and speak more specifically. Such choices lead him to new life in which he can accept himself in his own uniqueness and allow love and relationship to enter effectively into his life.

Phil's meetings with Ginny created a conflict between what he thought he ought to be (a celibate priest) and what he was actually experiencing (his own sexual feelings and attraction for Ginny). This conflict fostered a climate in which Phil could enter into a unique and personal relationship with God. At first, his love for Ginny was very painful, for it ruptured his concept of God and his image of self. He had known God to be Judge and Lawgiver; he had known himself to be a faithful and good man. His new experience of love destroys the world he had built for himself. On the positive side, as he grows in relationship with Ginny, he finds himself becoming more human and understanding in his dealing with others.

A poor self-image keeps Betty and Pete from fully accepting themselves. Whatever reinforces their feelings of inadequacy and guilt is not from God. Whatever leads them to dwell on the positive, to be kind to themselves, and to accept their own goodness—i.e., whatever helps them claim themselves and their own individuality—is from the good spirit.

Betty's negative judgments of herself control her so much that she may never come to hear the voice of the Lord as one who loves her personally and uniquely. Therapy provides some hope for freedom.

Pete's process of growth has been gradual and normal. He has risked believing in himself despite his father's desires that he choose a different vocation. He has felt supported by God in this risk and, to some extent, has trusted it as the voice of the Lord. But this trust is very fragile and continually vulnerable to the negative voices which would speak of his lack of self-worth. The choice to move south can provide the opportunity of claiming his identity and of growth into a personal relationship with God if he believes in both his father's love and God's love for him despite this action.

Phil, Betty, and Pete make choices out of principles, following universal laws or the laws of a given group. In their better moments they do for others what they would want others to do for them. Each one grows as he begins to make choices out of a sense of personal reality (their own, others', and God's). To use Kierkegaard's terms, each one is beginning to make the leap to the level of religious faith.

Mark, Shirley, and Janet operate out of faith or out of a sense of a personal relationship with God. Each represents a different stage in the life of development in faith.

In living a life of faith a person trusts that God is active and revelative in his life. The person senses God's presence uniquely and particularly in his life. Mark has just begun to enjoy God's presence in his life. Positive voices call him to accept and dwell in the uniqueness of God's love for him. Negative voices, especially those of fear, undermine his sense of self-confidence. The cutting edge of growth for Shirley is pretty much the same as that of Mark, except that she is being called to accept the negative dimension of herself as being loved by God. Positive voices summon her not to run from sin and darkness but to wait on the Lord's revelation. She receives a grace at the level of her being: God loves her unconditionally, even in her sinfulness.

Janet's choices, too, reveal the type of growth she is

experiencing. She acknowledges her strengths and weaknesses in her interview with Tomás. She freely entrusts herself to her spiritual director, to Eduardo, and to the people. The voices toward life call her to be open and vulnerable in her relationships. She is traversing the path to growth in intimacy that Erikson speaks of. This path leads to growth in relationship with the human Jesus and with the Jesus who is present in the poor.

As Janet continues to bond herself to the people, especially after she has felt humiliated and rejected by the people, her choices take on a specifically Paschal dimension. She allows humanity—her own and others—to form a part of her decision-making. She can accept others taking the leadership role and stand in the background. Though she finds the misunderstanding painful, she can let it fade into the background as she keeps her eyes on the goals: the freedom of the people, their sense of dignity, the reality of justice, and love. She can make the choice to forgive and be compassionate, accepting the weakness, limitations, and sinfulness that generally accompany our human endeavors to love and communicate. She chooses to overcome her fears of being rejected and hurt again because she values love and justice more than her own suffering. She trusts more easily in the unknown, knowing that God is Lord of all. In other words, she reacts comfortably with the living and dying that comprises a life of love and growth in faith.

The deep peace that Janet experiences even in difficult and tumultuous circumstances is rooted in relationship: in the goodness of herself, in the goodness of the people, in God who she knows is Love, and in Jesus who was and is fully human. She knows God is alive in all her experiences and that

Jesus—fully human and also fully divine—permeates all of reality. She does not always have to recognize God's presence consciously, for this realization now forms part of the fiber of her very being. She manifests the Paschal Mystery in self-denial (letting go her fears, her need to succeed and be thought well of) and in enablement (the countless ways that she chooses to love and be present to the people without counting the cost).

Role of the spiritual director

The role of the spiritual director changes as the person develops. Prior to a person's claiming identity, the director often speaks very directly. He functions somewhat like a teacher. The director keeps encouraging those who have not yet claimed themselves, such as Teresa, Phil, Betty, and Pete. He provides a stability which allows the person to risk being different by going against his fears. Often he provides an objective sounding board for the person's subjectivity and goodness. He teaches the ways of God's love and embodies that love in his own love and acceptance of the person.

Teresa needs stability and discipline. A strong director, who can say "no" to her whims and give her helpful patterns to embody responsibility in her life, can be very helpful. Teresa needs to be encouraged to choose to let go her fears that her pain will overwhelm her.

Betty and Pete especially need to be helped to claim their own goodness and to focus on the positive, since both focus primarily on the negative in themselves, Betty exceedingly so. Pete can appreciate in a freeing way any humor which highlights his negative appraisal of self.

Phil is more difficult to direct than the other three, because he continually tries to earn love and to prove his own goodness to himself. These efforts generally roam in his unconscious and rarely come to the surface. The trusting relationship of a mentor can encourage him to risk, to be specific, to own his feelings, and to claim his own experience. A young person of principle more readily trusts a mentor; the middle-aged or elderly person of principle finds it difficult to trust another. Even with a strong, trusting, mentor relationship, the passage to the realm of faith is difficult. Because the person of principle relies so much on his own intellectual understanding, he can control his thoughts and feelings, such that he mouths the words of accepting his own goodness without really letting love and relationship penetrate the core of his being. A wise director will recognize authentic lived faith when it happens and be tolerant of the intellectual understanding of faith which may antecede the gift of faith. Often, as in the case of Phil, a traumatic event provides the circumstances that allow the director to help the person of principle claim his own uniqueness and God's unique love for him.

The director's role changes from teacher to guide after the person has begun to claim his or her own identity. Mark is one of the easiest persons to be with in direction. His youthful enthusiasm of experiencing love is contagious. As a guide, Sr. Barbara fosters wonder, praise, and gratitude; she keeps Mark focused on the positive and God's love, helping him resist the temptation to yield to his past doubts of self. She also clarifies his fears of letting himself be freely loved.

Shirley is more difficult to accompany, and, unless the director has himself experienced the grace of being loved as a sinner, he will probably be ineffective. At times the circumstances summon him to be a teacher, at other times a guide, and at still other times a companion. He may teach discernment of spirits and how to recognize the Lord's presence in desolation. Often he teaches God's purpose in darkness and desolation. But he functions primarily as a guide. He keeps the person from running from the darkness and cautions him to wait for God's revelation. He points the person to the Lord on the cross in the darkness and suggests that he savor the Lord's mercy after the experience of freedom. In some of the darkest moments, he just simply companions the person.

As a person grows in the spiritual life, the role of his spiritual director changes to becoming a companion. The Spirit takes over and leads; the director watches and accompanies the journey. He feels especially privileged as the person grows in union with Jesus and His people and yields more to the action of Paschal Mystery in his life. The director becomes more a guide at the time of temptation and may help in discerning spirits. He may at times call the person to focus on the Lord in times of doubt, but generally the person will do this for himself. He may provide feedback for specific decisions. But, most often, he fades into the background as the Spirit leads.

The spiritual quest

The deepest desires of a person embody the spiritual quest. This book has described seven passages of growth in faith which comprise the spiritual quest. A person traverses these passages under the inspiration of grace.

Growth in faith does not correlate to age; some advance very quickly, others stagnate. Often a person rests some time at a particular stage of growth or resists moving through a particular passage. At times a person reverts to the security of a previous level of growth. Often a person experiences a foretaste of what lies ahead before he begins to engage seriously in appropriating a particular stage of faith development.

Inadequate notions of God as Lawgiver, Giver of Pleasure, and Punisher antecede a personal loving relationship with God. Obedience to an abstract philosophical God who is Truth, Love, Justice, and the Good can accompany these notions. A person may live at the moral-ethical level for a long time. Such a person often exudes his innate goodness; but a life lived too long at this level generally has negative consequences, such as perfectionism, Pelagianism, and self-righteousness.

The spiritual quest takes a quantum leap when one recognizes God as lovingly and personally involved in his life. One relates to God, person-to-person. He experiences God as having created him uniquely and as having loved him totally—even in his sinfulness.

The spiritual quest does not end in the acceptance of being loved—powerful though this grace be. A person desires to respond—however poorly—to the love he has received. God's grace reveals the passages the person traverses through the person of Jesus. A person finds God through being fully human as Jesus was and through loving despite the cost. In identifying with Jesus in his Paschal Mystery, a person discovers the richness of God's love. Faith in Jesus in His Paschal Mystery is the heart of our faith. It embodies compassion and sacrificial love, uniting a person both with God and with his neighbor.